USDA   United States Department of Agriculture

I0411761

Toward Robust Estimation of the Components of Forest Population Change: Simulation Results

Francis A. Roesch

Forest Service
Research & Development, Southern Research Station
e-General Technical Report SRS-194, July 2014

The Author:

Francis A. Roesch is a Research Mathematical Statistician,
Southern Research Station, U.S. Department of Agriculture
Forest Service, Asheville, NC 28804-3454.

July 2014
Southern Research Station
200 W.T. Weaver Blvd.
Asheville, NC 28804

www.srs.fs.usda.gov

Toward Robust Estimation of the Components of Forest Population Change: Simulation Results

Francis A. Roesch

CONTENTS

Toward Robust Estimation of the Components of Forest Population Change: Simulation Results

Francis A. Roesch

Abstract

This report presents the full simulation results of the work described in Roesch (2014), in which multiple levels of simulation were used to test the robustness of estimators for the components of forest change. In that study, a variety of spatial-temporal populations were created based on, but more variable than, an actual forest monitoring dataset, and then those populations were sampled under four sets of sampling error structure. An estimator modification was shown, to be used when extraneously obtained information indicated that a deviation to the assumed population model existed. The extraneous information was also incorporated into a mixed estimator. The first three approaches, without the incorporation of extraneous information, are compatible with large monitoring efforts that require intervention-free results. The mixed estimation approach accounts for model assumptions that sometimes remain latent in other approaches and is amenable to the formal incorporation of the extraneously obtained information. All four approaches were shown to work well when the sampling error structure was unbiased, while some notable differences in performance were observed at the temporal extremities of observation, in the presence of temporal anomalies, and in the presence of biased sampling error structures. Only those results necessary to make the salient points were presented in Roesch (2014). Full results are presented here both for full disclosure and for the reader interested in a more detailed understanding of the effects of realistic sampling errors on temporal estimates.

Keywords: Annual inventories, components of change, forest monitoring, sampling error, spatial-temporal sample design.

INTRODUCTION

The robustness of the estimation system for large-scale forest inventory and monitoring systems is an extremely important consideration. An estimation system is robust when it provides significant revelations about the conditions being investigated, even in the presence of violations of population and sampling error assumptions. This report gives the full results of a study that used two levels of simulation, the first to create a variety of spatial-temporal populations based on actual forest monitoring data and the second to sample those populations under a variety of sampling error structures. The author believes

that there is an education available to the energetic reader through a study of this full set of results that could not be conveyed in a single journal article. While reviewing the full set of results, the reader should keep in mind the differing effects of both overt and latent population trends in conjunction with a sometimes unknown sampling error structure on the assumptions underlying the various estimators. Using the components of change in this study facilitates understanding for the simple reason that the population trends of the components differ from each other for a common population and sampling error structure. In real inventories and monitoring efforts, the true population trends are never known, as they are in these simulations. The results will show how reasonably argued trend estimators can produce differing results and how those differing results can be used to infer underlying latent trends. The results also show a difficult reality in trend estimation: often the strength that is garnered from temporally adjacent observations will result in overly smooth estimates of trend. Additionally, it can often be beneficial to use a more sophisticated approach and include information from alternative sources.

Initially, I examine the robustness of three estimators for annual components of forest change when the temporal scale of the population estimand of interest is finer than the scale of observation in a temporally rotating panel sample design, such as the design used by the U.S. Department of Agriculture (USDA) Forest Service's Forest Inventory and Analysis (FIA) Program (Bechtold and Patterson 2005). The approaches are similar but differ in their underlying trend assumptions, leading to differences in how measurement intervals that are not centered on a target year inform the estimate for the target year. Next, a modification to these approaches shown in Roesch (2014), for use when extraneously obtained information indicates that a deviation to the assumed trend model has occurred, is evaluated. Finally, mixed estimation is used to package the extraneous information with a compatibility model. I show how conflicting results in the estimators can be used in an estimation system to reveal violations of the investigator's preconceived notions of both population trends and relationships and the structure of sampling errors.

The two major components of forest change that are of interest when monitoring a dynamic landscape are:

(1) Land use change during the period of interest in the form of reversion from some other land use to forest, and diversion away from forest to some other land use, and

(2) Change of trees on land that is forested during the entire period of interest.

Due to the cost constraints present in all forest monitoring efforts, neither of these components is ever fully observed. For a dynamic forest inventory to be sufficiently informative, however, it is important to acknowledge the distinction between land use change and the change that occurs on forest land. Both are important factors when evaluating the state of the forests in an area or nation, but the full implications of the distinction are often lost in aggregations of national forest inventory (NFI) data. That is, (1) and (2) above are somewhat confounded. The discussion below assumes that there exists a method of grouping land into subsets according to the temporal period of forest land classification, within the temporal period of interest. The methods discussed here can then be applied to the subsets individually. Van Deusen and Roesch (2009) and Roesch and Van Deusen (2012) explored estimation of the change in forest land classification, in the context of the NFI in the United States. Roesch (2014) and this paper concentrate on estimation of the change in the tree population on forest land.

Historically, the definitions of the components of growth were sample dependent. The resulting quantities could easily be calculated from remeasured samples but were not truly estimates of population parameters. Eriksson (1995) corrected this deficiency with the presentation of a set of definitions for the continuous components of change. Roesch (2007b) presented a discrete version of the Eriksson definitions, which are used here.

The population components of change are compatible; that is:

$$\mathbf{Y}_{t+1} = \mathbf{Y}_t + \mathbf{L}_{t,t+1} + \mathbf{E}_{t,t+1} - \mathbf{M}_{t,t+1} - \mathbf{H}_{t,t+1} \qquad (1)$$

where

$\mathbf{Y}_t$ = the value of interest at time t

$\mathbf{L}_{t,t+1}$ = growth in the value of interest on live trees between time t and time $t+1$

$\mathbf{E}_{t,t+1}$ = the value of interest on live trees as they enter the population between time t and time $t+1$

$\mathbf{M}_{t,t+1}$ = the value of interest on trees as they die between time t and time $t+1$

$\mathbf{H}_{t,t+1}$ = the value of interest on trees as they are harvested between time t and time $t+1$

Without loss of generality, in this paper, the value of interest is cubic meter volume and the entry criterion is 12.7 cm at 1.37 m above the ground (diameter at breast height, or d.b.h.).

Consider a sample design that consists of g mutually exclusive, spatially disjoint temporal panels in which, subsequent to a random areal start, one panel per year is measured, in turn, for g consecutive years. After each cycle, the panel measurement sequence reinitiates. Such a design is used by the USDA Forest Service's FIA Program and discussed in Bechtold and Patterson (2005) and Roesch (2007b). Consequently, in a five-panel system, the five panels are measured for growth over a 10-year period. That is, panel 1 is measured in years 1 and 6, panel 2 is measured in years 2 and 7, etc. Several philosophies have emerged as to how data resulting from this design should be applied to estimates of growth and change because remeasurement of the panels provides observations that are spatially disjoint but temporally overlapping, and the temporal scale of the population of interest is finer than the scale of observation. Roesch (2007b) argued that the average annual growth within each individual panel is best applied to the center of the measurement interval, which is analogous to an assumption of linear change between observations. All analytical methods proposed to date for this class of sample designs for forest monitoring have been predicated on this or similar assumptions. This assumption also applies to most of the discussion below. However, I do explore the effects of a simple nonconforming population trend, which can be either latent or overt.

ESTIMATORS FOR THE COMPONENTS OF CHANGE

It is often argued that estimators of these components of change should be compatible because the components themselves are compatible. In this report, I compare four general approaches for estimating the components of forest change. In the first three approaches, each component is estimated independently of the others. In the fourth approach, the estimates are constrained to be compatible. Assume that the estimands of interest are the m^3 volume/ha of all live trees in a fixed area in each component of change category during each year of a multi-decadal period.

The first estimation approach uses a Centralized Difference Estimator (CDE), the second uses the Exponentially Weighted Difference (EWD) estimator of Roesch (2007a), the third uses the (semi-centralized) Moving-Window Mean of Ratios (MWMOR) estimator in Roesch and Van Deusen (2013), and the fourth uses the mixed estimator variant in Roesch (2007a). Because we know that compatibility will have a cost in terms of squared error loss for one or more of the estimated components, the initial results compare only the first three approaches. The fourth approach is discussed in a situation in which the first three approaches, lacking the benefit of extraneous information, are shown to give unfavorable results.

I first present three estimators that can be expected to yield equivalent results until they are differentially affected when an underlying assumption becomes tenuous. When an anomaly occurs that can be expected to affect these estimators under the given sample design, I apply a reweighting scheme in order to incorporate extraneously obtained information. Subsequently, the extraneously obtained weights are incorporated directly into a mixed estimator, and all four estimators are tested in the anomalous situation.

Centralized Difference Estimator

The Centralized Difference Estimator is a moving average estimator applied to a series of equally weighted within-panel differences (i.e., a series of change component values). In the CDE, a panel difference is applied to the center interval (or year) and combined with adjoining panel differences. Let:

$\overline{d}_{h+t,h+1}$ = the annual mean of a remeasured panel difference, such as $t^{-1}\hat{L}_{h+t,h+1}$, and

$r = (m-1)/2$, where m is odd and is the number of remeasured panels used in the estimator.

Then the CDE for component C in year k is:

$$C_k^{CDE} = m^{-1} \sum_{i=-r}^{r} \overline{d}_{k+r+i,k-r+i} \qquad (2)$$

The CDE provides no estimates for m years on each end of the time string. In practice, an ad hoc variation would have to be used in order to provide some or all of these

estimates. Here, five panels are used in the estimator when there are differences from at least two panels available before and after the central panel. Three panels are used in the estimator when there is only one additional panel difference available on either side of the central panel (e.g., for the second and penultimate estimates). A single panel difference is used for the first and the final estimates.

Exponentially Weighted Difference Estimator

The Exponentially Weighted Difference estimator of Roesch (2007a) is similar in concept to the exponentially weighted moving average (EWMA) estimator common in the quality control literature (Chandra 2000), and the econometrics literature (West and Harrison 1989, p. 55). In the EWD estimator, a series of differences (i.e., a series of change component values) within panels is calculated. The EWD estimator gives larger weights to the interval observations closest to the interval of interest, allowing more temporally local variation than if equal weights are used. The panel difference is applied to the central annual interval and combined with the m-1 adjoining interval differences. The supporting panels are down-weighted exponentially with each step away from the central interval. In addition to the notation above for the CDE, let:

$$\alpha = \left(\frac{r}{r+1}\right)$$

The EWD estimator for component C in year y is:

$$C_y^{EWD} = \sum_{i=-r}^{r} \frac{(1-\alpha)}{\left(1+\alpha-2\alpha^{r+1}\right)} \alpha^{|i|} \overline{d}_{y+r+i,y-r+i} \qquad (3)$$

As with the CDE, the EWD estimator also does not provide estimates for m years on each end of the time string, and I use the same solution for these extraneous years. That is, three panels are used in the estimator when there are differences from at least one panel available before and after the central panel. A single panel difference is used otherwise, rendering the EWD estimator equal to the CDE when there is only one panel difference available.

Moving-Window Mean of Ratios Estimator

Roesch and Van Deusen (2013) proposed an estimator that arose from a different perspective from the two estimators above that I apply to the current objective, as fully explained in Roesch (2014). The idea was simple: one stacks the observations on a temporal scale (or a function of the temporal scale), and then slices through the stack (say to create annual segments) to determine how much of each observation contributes to the estimate for each year. For this problem, as in Roesch and Van Deusen (2013), time is rescaled relative to the proportion of the growing season elapsed within each year. The change components are modeled between observations to allocate the components to the years in which the change is assumed to have occurred. A simple time-adjusted estimator for annual volume growth (within the live growth component) is the MWMOR estimator for component C in year y:

$$C_y^{MWMOR} = \frac{1}{n_y} \sum_{i=1}^{n_y} \frac{c_{i,y}}{p_{i,y}} \qquad (4)$$

where

n_y = the number of plots observing growth in year y

$P_{i,y}$ = the product of portion of year y growing season observed by plot i and the portion of plot i area within the area of interest

$c_{i,y}$ = the value of component C observed on plot i, assignable to year y.

Incorporating Outside Information

Situations arise within the scope of national-scale forest monitoring efforts for which the data obtained from the sample design are inadequate. Many approaches to incorporating extraneous information in forest inventories have been proposed and proven useful for particular applications. A weighting method given in Roesch (2014) can be used in conjunction with each of the estimators above, and with the mixed estimator below to incorporate extraneous information.

Assume that there exists strong external information that the expected value of X at time t, $E(X_t)$, differs from the expected value of a previous estimate of X, $E(\hat{x}_t^p)$, at time t by a factor kw. For the estimators above, this information suggests a reweighting of previous estimates for all estimates that had relied on the previous estimate for time t. Let:

$$kv = kw + n_t - 1 \qquad (5)$$

where

n_t = the number of years used for each annual estimate, and let

$$kt^- = n_t / kv \qquad (6)$$

and

$$kt = (nt * kw) / kv \qquad (7)$$

Then weight the previous estimates at times other than time t that used the previous time t estimate by kt^-, and weight previous estimates at time t by kt to form the reweighted estimates.

Mixed Estimation

The mixed estimator (Theil 1963) can be used to draw strength from overlapping panels and easily incorporate extraneous information into forest monitoring efforts. Mixed estimation was first proposed for use in forestry when Korhonen (1993) used the method for calibrating tree volume functions. Van Deusen (1996, 1999, 2000) developed mixed estimators for annual forest inventory designs, and Roesch (2007a) used it for components of change estimation. In Roesch (2014), mixed estimation is used as a convenient way to incorporate both (1) a belief in how the individual growth components should be related and transition from year to year, and (2) extraneous information that suggests that a modification to those beliefs is appropriate. To achieve these goals, start with the three transition models below, and then adapt those models to incorporate the extraneous information. The three base models all assume compatibility of the total annual change with the components of change; that is, for each year t:

$$\delta_{t,t+1} = \hat{V}_{t+1} - \hat{V}_t = \hat{L}_{t,t+1} + \hat{E}_{t,t+1} - \hat{M}_{t,t+1} - \hat{H}_{t,t+1} \qquad (8)$$

Initially, Model 1 assumes that for each component $C = L, E, M,$ or H, at each time t:

$$\hat{C}_{t,t+1} - \hat{C}_{t+1,t+2} = \varepsilon_{C,t} \qquad (9)$$

Model 2 assumes that for each component, at each time t:

$$\hat{C}_{t,t+1} - 2\hat{C}_{t+1,t+2} + \hat{C}_{t+2,t+3} = \varepsilon_{C,t} \qquad (10)$$

while Model 3 assumes that for each component, at each time t:

$$\hat{C}_{t,t+1} - 3\hat{C}_{t+1,t+2} + 3\hat{C}_{t+2,t+3} - \hat{C}_{t+3,t+4} = \varepsilon_{C,t} \qquad (11)$$

Formulation of the constraints under each of these models is straightforward.

Next, let:

$\mathbf{Y}$ = an $(n_c * n_t)$ row x n_s column response matrix

where

n_c = 5, which is the number of growth components plus 1

n_t = the number of years in the estimation interval

n_s = the sample size for all n_p panels.

The columns of **Y** are arranged in n_t successive ordered 5-tuples of (1) the MWMOR estimate of annual change, (2) observed annual live growth, (3) entry, (4) mortality, and (5) harvest, for each year in the observation interval for a plot and zeroes otherwise.

A user's level of belief in the underlying model can be incorporated into the mixed estimator in several ways. Here, as explained in Roesch (2014), I choose to preprocess **Y** by first reweighting according to the extraneous information, adapting the constraint matrix, and then strictly applying the constraints to ensure growth component compatibility. To accomplish this weighting for estimates at times other than time t that use estimates for time t, weight the time t estimate by kw^{-1} before combining with the non-time t estimates. For estimates at time t, weight the non-time t estimates by kw before combining with the time t estimate. Indicate the outside information-weighted response matrix as $\mathbf{Y}_{OI}$. Then let:

$\mathbf{\Sigma}$ = an (n_c*n_t) row x (n_c*n_t) column variance/co-variance matrix of $\mathbf{Y}_{OI}$

$\mathbf{R}$ = an (n_R) row x (n_c*n_t) column constraint matrix, appropriate for a given model

where

n_R = the number of constraint rows

$\hat{\boldsymbol{\beta}}$ = an (n_c*n_t) row x 1 column predictive coefficient vector for strict constraints:

$$\hat{\boldsymbol{\beta}} = \mathbf{Y}_{OI} - \left[\mathbf{\Sigma}\mathbf{R}'\left(\mathbf{R}\mathbf{\Sigma}\mathbf{R}'\right)^{-1} \mathbf{R}\mathbf{Y}_{OI} \right] \quad (12)$$

Let **M** be an (n_c*n_t) row x n_s column matrix, with each column consisting of n_t repetitions of the vector $(n_s^{-1}, n_s^{-1}n_p, n_s^{-1}n_p, n_s^{-1}n_p, n_s^{-1}n_p)$. Then:

$$\hat{\mathbf{Y}}_{mix} = \hat{\boldsymbol{\beta}}\mathbf{M}' \quad (13)$$

SIMULATIONS

The exact details of the simulations used to both create the populations and obtain the error-included samples are given in Roesch (2014). Here I emphasize the philosophy behind the simulations and contend that the approach used is unique in the forestry literature in its completeness of consideration of errors in forest monitoring efforts. That is not to say that a more varied set of error structures for both the population creation and sampling simulations would not be appropriate, but it is to say that each of these steps is usually incomplete. Usually when the focus is on comparing either sampling methods or estimators, construction of realistic and diverse populations is given inadequate consideration. In addition, painstaking efforts are usually made to take design-unbiased samples in the sampling simulations, whereas in actual monitoring efforts a plethora of errors occurs, rendering the sample design a mere model of the realized sample. Unless the level of effort in each of these simulation steps is at least as high as it is in this study, the robustness of an estimation system cannot be fully evaluated.

Population Simulations

In this application, I use FIA data collected in South Carolina from 1998 through 2011 to construct five simulated populations. Although all of the populations are plausible, the intention was for the first population (Population 0) to be a seed population using the simplest possible model for deriving annual values from multiyear observations. The seed population allows the simulation of a series of populations, some of which we might assume to be like the one from which the sample data were drawn, and others that might arise from a wider diversity of conditions.

I created the five simulated populations by first selecting all remeasured forested plots spanning the 14-year period from the South Carolina data. Most of the resulting 2,430 forested plots had three measurement times (i.e., two observed growth intervals for each component). As explained more fully in Roesch (2014), the observations were converted to annual values for each year in the 14-year period to create Set 1, and the construction of Population 0 was then obtained from 600 variance-interjected copies of Set 1, resulting in a population of 1,458,000 ha. Specifically, the variance was interjected at two steps. In step 1, to keep the existing trend and add variance to the seed, variance was interjected by multiplying all values for each component on each ha by a random variate, unique for that ha, drawn from an N(1, 0.025) distribution. In step 2, variance was introduced temporally by multiplying the result of step 1, for each annual value for each component on each ha, by a unique random variate drawn from an N(1, 0.0025) distribution. Because the sampling simulation "observes" 5-year intervals, rather than the annual values, the manner of population construction should not unduly influence the results. However, to reduce further any potential linear effect, a mild (latent) nonlinear trend was introduced into each of the components in Population 1.

For Population 2, a mild nonlinear trend was introduced into the components of live growth, entry, and mortality, and a stronger nonlinear trend was introduced into the harvest component in order to simulate increasing harvesting pressure. For Population 3, a mild nonlinear trend was introduced into the components of live growth, entry, and harvest, and a catastrophic high mortality event (of four times the mortality rate of Population 1) was introduced for the year 2004. Population 4 was initially as in Population 1 and then postulated climate change effects were simulated by increasing mortality and decreasing growth and recruitment, with harvest levels remaining the same. Each of the five populations consists of 1,458,000 forested "hectares" or "elements" with measurable cubic meter volume at some time in the 14-year period. The five populations were constructed to examine estimator performance and robustness in the presence of plausible suboptimal population characteristics, for the given sample design and sampling error structure.

Sampling Simulations

Usually, the overriding criterion for selection of an estimator in forest inventories is the minimum mean squared error for the candidate unbiased estimators. Rarely considered is the effect of sampling error in the form of bias on the robustness of theoretically unbiased estimators. Some notable exceptions have been Gertner (1987), Thomas and Roesch (1990), Eastaugh and Hasenauer (2013), and Roesch (2014). In this investigation, estimator robustness was tested in a simulation by sampling each population under four different assumptions of total sampling error structure. The models are intended to represent all error that would not be addressed by the use of an unbiased sampling simulation. The unbiased simulation might be the closest one can come to the pure sampling error inherent in a perfectly observed and measured sample, while in a realized sample there could also be "item observation" errors, frame errors, and measurement errors to say the least. That is, the error structure models used here are intended to represent all of the ways that a realized sample might differ from its perfectly observed theoretical counterpart.

A complete description of the construction of the error structures is given in Roesch (2014). In brief, for Error Structure 1, sampling error was assumed to consist exclusively of a small variance, effected by multiplying a unique random normal deviate of mean 1 and standard deviation 0.025 by each sampled observation of each component. For Error Structure 2, I assumed that sampling error consisted of a small variance and a positive bias on all change components. I effected Error Structure 2 by multiplying a unique random normal

deviate of mean 1.05 and standard deviation of 0.025 by each observation of each component.

I assumed that sampling error consisted of variance and positive bias on volume, live growth, and entry, and a negative bias on harvest and mortality for Error Structure 3. I effected Error Structure 3 thus: each observation of live growth and entry was multiplied by a unique random normal deviate of mean 1.05 and standard deviation of 0.025. Each observation of mortality and harvest was multiplied by a unique random normal deviate of mean 0.90 and standard deviation of 0.025. Although the level of simulated error is somewhat arbitrary, errors of approximately these magnitudes seem reasonable based on the work in Thomas and Roesch (1990) and the results in Eastaugh and Hasenauer (2013).

Error Structure 4 was similar to Error Structure 3, but I assumed that sampling error consisted of a higher variance and greater bias, as follows. Each observation of live growth and entry was multiplied by a unique random normal deviate of mean 1.1 and standard deviation of 0.05. Each observation of mortality and harvest was multiplied by a unique random normal deviate of mean 0.80 and standard deviation of 0.05.

For Population 3, I also simulated the availability of extraneously obtained information that mortality during 2004 was about four times higher than in surrounding years by drawing a random variate from a Normal distribution of mean 4, and standard deviation of 0.05, and setting it equal to kw for each observation. Then estimates for each estimator—the CDE, the EWD estimator, and the MWMOR estimator—were reweighted to obtain the CDE-OI, the EWD-OI estimator, and the MWMOR-OI estimator. The -OI suffix for each estimator indicates the inclusion of outside information, as described in Roesch (2014). The input values and constraints for the mixed estimator models were reweighted analogously.

Each simulation consisted of 1,000 iterations of 1,000 plots each (without replacement) from each population, under each of the four sampling error structures. For each year, I calculated the Empirical Bias (EB) and the Empirical Mean Squared Error (EMSE) over the 1,000 iterations, between each estimator and the true population values under each of the four error structures.

That is:

$$EB_{PES} = \frac{1}{1000} \sum_{i=1}^{1000} \left(\hat{x}_{PESi} - X_P \right) \tag{14}$$

where

$\hat{x}_{PESi}$ is the sample estimate of X in population P for estimator E, under error structure S for iterate i. Likewise:

$$EMSE_{PES} = \frac{1}{1000} \sum_{i=1}^{1000} \left(\hat{x}_{PESi} - X_P \right)^2 \qquad (15)$$

Usually, the overriding criterion for selection of an estimator in forest inventories is the minimum mean squared error for the candidate unbiased estimators. This priority might suggest that the presentation of these results should focus on *EMSE*. Because the four error structures were devised to examine estimator performance over these populations in the presence of plausible differentially biased sampling error, the reader should pay special attention to the *EB* in the results. On the other hand, the reader should not be overly influenced by an extremely low *EB* result because it can occur when sampling bias is being counteracted by estimation bias.

RESULTS

Tables 0 through 4 give the distribution statistics for 1999-2011, for Populations 0 through 4, respectively. When examining the results of Populations 0 and 1, the reader should recall that Population 0 was constructed from 600 variance-interjected copies of Set 1, in a manner that should reduce the artificial linearity introduced by constructing the annual populations from multiyear observations. That is, Population 0 could be viewed as the result of the minimal prima facie effort to build a realistic annual population from the data arising from panelized multiyear observation intervals. To reduce further any potential linear effect in the annual time-series, a mild (latent) nonlinear trend was introduced into each of the components in Population 1. For Population 2, a mild nonlinear trend was introduced into the components of live growth, entry, and mortality, and a stronger nonlinear trend was introduced into the harvest component, in order to simulate increasing harvesting pressure. For Population 3, a mild nonlinear trend was introduced into the components of live growth, entry, and harvest, and a catastrophic high mortality event (of four times the mortality rate of Population 1) was introduced for the year 2004. Postulated climate change effects were simulated in Population 4 by increasing mortality and decreasing growth and recruitment, relative to Population 1, with harvest levels remaining the same. The five tables of statistics for the populations can give the reader a fuller understanding of the breadth of trend effects and anomalies that existed to challenge the robustness of the estimators.

The sampling simulation results are given in three figures for each combination of population and sampling error structure. The twenty combinations of population and sampling error structure are therefore given in sixty

figures, labeled as figure *pe*M, *pe*B, and *pe*E for the mean, bias, and mean squared error, respectively, for population *p* and Error Structure *e*. Each graph plots the corresponding statistics for the CDE, the EWD estimator, and the MWMOR estimator, by growth component for estimation years 2000 through 2009. These are the years that are the center of at least one observation window (or panel), for a sample drawn under this design from a population spanning 1998-2001.

Population 0

Figures 0*e*M, 0*e*B, and 0*e*E, with *e* = 1, 2, 3, or 4, give the empirical mean, bias, and mean squared error, respectively, over 1,000 iterations of 1,000 samples each from Population 0 under Sampling Error Structure *e*. As proposed above, Population 0 could be viewed as the result of the minimal prima facie effort to build a realistic annual population from the data arising from panelized multiyear observation intervals.

Error Structure 1—Recall that, for Error Structure 1, sampling error was assumed to consist exclusively of a small variance, resulting in an unbiased sampling simulation, representing the pure sampling error inherent in a perfectly observed and measured sample. Therefore, figures 01M, 01B, and 01E give the results that would be achieved through the usual assumptions made in estimator comparisons.

All three estimators, in conjunction with the design, are shown to be general smoothers. That is, the design observes 5-year windows, thereby providing an average annual change or "smoothing" the actual annual change. The estimators, while drawing strength from overlapping panels, provide further smoothing. In figure 01M, this effect can be clearly seen in all four components, under this simplest sampling error structure. It is also seen in all of the simulation mean graphs of these results.

Five panels of data are used for all of the estimators for estimates of the central estimation years 2002 through 2007. As expected, owing to the nonlinear latent trends, the EWD is sometimes slightly closer to the population value than the other estimators are in these central years.

By definition, the CDE and the EWD estimator use the observations from a single panel's remeasurement for years 2000 and 2009 while the noncentralized MWMOR estimator uses the observations from three panels. The CDE and the EWD estimator use the observations from the remeasurement of three panels for years 2001 and 2008 while the semi-centralized MWMOR estimator uses the observations from four panels for these years. In the temporal extremes, the results for the MWMOR estimator are mixed, with the expected bias due to the use of the off-center panels sometimes (such as in live growth and mortality for 2009), but not always, being overridden by the lower variance from the larger sample. This outcome can be verified by comparing the harvest and mortality results in figures 01B and 01E.

Confounded with this variance-bias tradeoff effect is an off-center effect in the MWMOR. Drawing the reader's attention to the mortality estimates for the years 2000 and 2001 in figures 01M, 01B, and 01E, and noting that the true population mean shown in figure 01M is unknown in an actual inventory, we can discuss how the use of multiple estimators can reveal underlying population phenomena. During these particular years, the MWMOR results appear superior by all measures and that is the conclusion that would be drawn by the usual methods of estimator comparison. In figure 01M the MWMOR estimates for 2000 and 2001 are much closer to the population mean than are the other two estimators. More important, however, is the relative association of the various estimators. The MWMOR estimates for 2000 and 2001 are lower than and have a lower slope than the corresponding estimates for the other two estimators. Additionally, the MWMOR estimate for 2000 is very close to the CDE and EWD estimates for 2001. This is because the three estimates use the same information in different ways. If all of the assumptions underlying any arguments for optimality for these three estimators were strictly true, this particular set of facts would not be in evidence. That is, the centralized three-panel estimates for 2001 for the CDE and EWD would be closer to the population mean for 2001, than the off-center three-panel MWMOR estimate for 2000 is to the population mean for 2000. The relative positioning of the estimates, as they exist, would tell us, in lieu of a plotted population mean line, that the slope of the mortality trend is increasing to the left (or decreasing as time progresses.). Therefore, the pattern or relative positioning of the estimates from the different estimators is revealing something about the underlying population that we would not necessarily know if we had favored and used a single estimator. As the reader progresses through the results for the various populations and sampling error structures, she or he should note that different combinations of population and error structure will result in different rankings of the estimators, but regular patterns between the estimators always indicate the same thing about the underlying trend.

Error Structure 2—Recall that in Error Structure 2, a positive sampling bias was interjected into all change components. The results can be seen by comparing the figures for Error Structure 2 with those for Error Structure 1. For instance all of the estimates in figure 02M are

higher than the corresponding estimates in figure 01M, but the trends for the individual estimators are virtually identical between the two figures. What may not be intuitively obvious is that sampling bias does not always result in estimates of higher bias. A comparison of figures 01B and 02B shows that for some components in certain years the bias created by the smoothing effect of the estimators is counteracted by the sampling bias. This offsetting effect is also reflected in lower empirical mean squared error values for the year 2000 entry estimates in figure 02E, for instance, relative to the corresponding values in figure 01E.

Error Structure 3—Sampling error consisted of variance and positive bias on volume, live growth, and entry, and a negative bias on harvest and mortality for Error Structure 3. The results for live growth and entry are therefore virtually identical for those components in figures 03M, 03B, and 03E to the the corresponding graphs in figures 02M, 02B, and 02E. Our interest lies in comparing the mortality and harvest results in figures 03M, 03B, and 03E, to the corresponding results in figures 01M, 01B, and 01E. The mortality and harvest results vary starkly due mostly to the different curvilinear population trends. Surprisingly, the overall estimates for mortality are slightly better under the negatively biased Error Structure 3 than they were for the unbiased Error Structure 1. The same cannot be said for the harvest estimates. The mortality estimates are somewhat better under negative bias due to the concave upward shape of the population curve. The harvest estimates, on the other hand, are worse under a negatively biased error structure due to the concave downward shape of that population curve.

Error Structure 4—Error structure 4 had higher variance and greater bias than Error Structure 3, with bias of the same sign for each component as Error Structure 3. The strong sampling bias effect of Error Structure 4 is easily observable by comparing the simulation mean graphs of figure 04M with those of figure 01M. However, note also in those comparisons that the trends for live growth, entry, and mortality would appear almost identical in those two figures if the population mean lines were not present, as they would not be in an actual inventory, and the y-axes were not labeled. That is, under both error structures, the conclusions that one would draw about trend would be the same, and those estimators appear robust for trend in those mildly curvilinear cases. Again, the same conclusion could not be drawn for harvest. The strong concave-downward curve resulted in most of the estimates having negative bias under unbiased sampling error structure, while the effect was greatly exacerbated under the strong negatively biased error structure.

Population 1

Figures 1eM, 1eB, and 1eE, with e = 1, 2, 3, or 4, give the empirical mean, bias, and mean squared error, respectively, over 1,000 iterations of 1,000 samples each from Population 1 under Sampling Error Structure e, by growth component for estimation years 2000 through 2009.

Population 1 was constructed similarly to Population 0 except that a mild (latent) nonlinear trend was introduced into each of the components to reduce further any potential linear effect resulting from the method of construction. By examining the results figures for Population 1, the reader can verify that the results for Population 1 are almost identical to the corresponding results for Population 0.

As with the same case in Population 0, the three figures for Error Structure 4 in general reflect the bias and greater variance of Error Structure 4 over Error Structure 1 for Population 1. The estimators do not appear to be differentially affected by the bias in Error Structure 4. I do note that occasionally the bias in the temporal extremities shown in figure 11B for the MWMOR estimator is offset in figure 14B by the counteracting bias in the sampling error structure, resulting in lower empirical mean squared error in figure 14E relative to figure 11E. This reinforces a point made in Eastaugh and Hasenauer (2013): often the implementation of theoretically unbiased sample designs will result in biased samples for a myriad of reasons, and estimators should therefore be evaluated in consideration of that possibility. With respect to robustness, note that if we were examining only the outcome for one or more of these estimators, and did not know the true population values (that is, the population line was missing from figures 11M and 14M), we would draw the same conclusions about the trend in each of the components. This consistency suggests that all of these estimators are, at least in this regard, robust.

Population 2

For Population 2, a mild nonlinear trend was introduced into the components of live growth, entry, and mortality, and a stronger nonlinear trend was introduced into the harvest component, in order to simulate increasing harvesting pressure. The increased harvesting pressure throughout the estimation period had subtle effects on the other change components. Close examination of the results for live growth, entry, and mortality for Population 2 should convince the reader that they are virtually identical to the corresponding results figures for Population 1. Although the increased harvesting pressure is seen in the Mean graphs for Population 2, the concave curvilinear shape of the population trend once again is the biggest factor in the results, and the resulting conclusions mimic exactly those reached in the previously discussed population graphs.

Population 3

For Population 3, a mild nonlinear trend was introduced into the components of live growth, entry, and harvest, and a catastrophic high mortality event (of four times the mortality rate of Population 1) was introduced for the year 2004.

Figures 34M, 34B, and 34E give the empirical mean, bias, and mean squared error, respectively, for 1,000 iterations of 1,000 samples each from Population 3 under Sampling Error Structure 4, for the CDE, the EWD estimator, and the MWMOR estimator, by growth component and estimation year. The most notable outcome for Population 3 under all error structures is that all three estimators give no indication of the extreme anomaly for mortality in 2004, due to the smoothing effects of both the sample design and the estimators applied to the outcomes of the design. The anomaly in 2004 is spread out over the estimates for the surrounding years, so the estimators reflect very high empirical bias and empirical mean squared error for mortality in 2004 in figures 34B and 34E, respectively. The sample design itself makes this single-year anomaly particularly difficult to evaluate, and impossible to definitively separate from a possible spatial effect.

Population 4

Population 4 was initially as in Population 1 and then postulated climate change effects were simulated by increasing mortality and decreasing growth and recruitment, with harvest levels remaining the same.

The empirical mean, bias, and mean squared error, respectively, for 1,000 iterations of 1,000 samples each from Population 4 under Sampling Error Structure 3, for the CDE, the EWD estimator, and the MWMOR estimator, by growth component and estimation year, are given in figures 43M, 43B, and 43E. Although Population 4 has a greater diversity of conditions than Population 1, the differences in estimator performance between figures 43M, 43B, and 43E, relative to the corresponding graphs in figures 11M, 11B, and 11E, appear to correspond to those that could be expected under the more severe Sampling Error Structure 3.

Population 3—With Outside Information

Figures 3MM, 3MB, and 3ME give the empirical mean, bias, and mean squared error, respectively, for 1,000 iterations of 1,000 samples each from Population 3 under Sampling Error Structures 1 through 4, for the estimators incorporating outside information, for the mortality component by estimation year. Although it is true that the outside information was not perfect, all of the estimators incorporating the outside information benefitted in the form of improved mortality estimates for the year 2004 and the surrounding years that used observations spanning 2004. Figure 3MM shows that under each of the sampling error structures each of the estimators exhibits a pattern very similar to the mortality trend for the population. The patterns differ from the population trend predictably by sampling error structure. Figure 3MB shows more clearly than figure 3MM that the order of the estimates for each year remains constant through the different sampling error structures, indicating that sampling error structure did not differentially affect the estimators. Some interaction between the outside information and sampling error structure is indicated by the position of the group of estimators for 2004 relative to the groups of estimators for the surrounding years. Figure 3ME shows that the empirical mean squared error results for the mixed estimator models are often, but not always, higher than they are for the other models. This effect could be viewed as the cost of compatibility.

CONCLUSIONS

I explored some special problems that arise in estimation of the components of change when the temporal scale of the population estimand of interest is finer than the scale of observation under both biased and unbiased sampling error structures. In the example simulations, the temporal scale of observation was 5 years while the temporal dimension of the population of interest was 1 year. All of the approaches worked well in the temporal mid-range of observations in the presence of smooth population trends, under unbiased sampling error structures. The smoothing aspect of the sample design and the estimators that did not use outside information was problematic when the sign of the slope of a trend changed. The maximum year and years surrounding it were under-predicted, while the minimum year and years surrounding it were over-predicted under unbiased sampling error. By interjecting a single year anomaly into Population 3, I presented an especially difficult (but realistic) situation given the sampling frame. The results of these more thorough simulations support the simulations and conclusions of Roesch (2007a) with

respect to comparisons between the EWD estimator and this application of the Mixed Estimator. The simulations also showed the variance/bias trade-off encountered when the MWMOR estimator was used in the extremity years of observation. Although the MWMOR estimator is sometimes biased in the presence of trend in the extremity years, the empirical mean-squared error was often lower than it was for the other estimators. Of the four general approaches for estimating the components of forest change from this annually rotating five-panel sample design (the Centralized Difference Estimator, the Exponentially Weighted Difference estimator, the Moving-Window Mean of Ratios estimator, and the Mixed Estimator), the first three approaches are very compatible with large monitoring efforts that require intervention-free results. These three simple approaches were shown to be amenable when outside information suggests an adaptation to the weighting scheme. The fourth approach, the mixed estimator, is also amenable to the incorporation of extraneously derived information and can easily incorporate complex models. No single estimation approach has (or could have) been shown to be a panacea, and some notable differences in performance were observed at the temporal extremities of observation, in the presence of temporal anomalies, and in the presence of biased sampling error structures. With respect to trend, all of the estimators are robust, but the CDE, the EWD estimator, and the MWMOR estimator are somewhat nonresponsive to highly variable trends, and all estimators are subject to the smoothing effect of the sample design considered here. This particular deficiency in the design was shown to be readily corrected through the incorporation of outside information.

This study suggests that one should probably not attempt to choose a single estimation approach in order to address the widest range of estimation objectives. The estimators considered here were shown to differ in their respective robustness to different, but realistic, underlying error structures, aspects of which may not always be known. Rather, an investigator would be well served to embrace the philosophy behind the Thomas and Roesch (1990) and Eastaugh and Hasenauer (2013) articles: when real data are involved, there is value in making estimates using as many theoretical approaches as possible. When different approaches produce similar results, there is strong evidence for those results. However, it can be even more informative when different (but defensible) approaches produce varied results. In that situation, it is incumbent upon the analyst to figure out why the varied results have occurred. Quite simply, an analyst should look at the data from as many angles as she or he has the time and energy for, in an attempt to understand fully the natural phenomena that are being imperfectly observed.

Table 0—Distribution Statistics for Population 0

Component	Statistic	Year												
		1999	2000	2001	2002	2003	2004	2005	2006	2007	2008	2009	2010	2011
Volume	Minimum	0	0	0	0	0	0	0	0	0	0	0	0	0
	1st Quartile	4.48	10.78	16.45	21.54	25.98	30.52	33.88	36.37	38.89	40.42	41.86	42.69	44.04
	Median	55.26	63.07	69.78	75.28	80.49	83.95	86.51	88.65	90.57	93.02	96.14	99.99	103.70
	Mean	81.92	87.45	92.68	97.18	101.35	105.13	108.23	110.63	112.65	114.66	117.31	120.53	124.62
	3rd Quartile	125.85	133.47	139.69	145.20	149.49	153.86	157.93	160.80	163.55	166.30	169.10	174.00	180.14
	Maximum	583.18	591.50	609.80	625.30	638.04	648.09	655.38	659.95	663.75	664.22	661.10	664.47	789.74
Live growth	Minimum	-5.72	-6.80	-42.60	-20.45	-10.48	-13.15	-22.14	-31.07	-23.06	-9.42	-10.28	-6.06	-11.56
	1st Quartile	0	0.42	1.08	1.52	1.88	1.84	1.69	1.22	0.48	0	0	0	0
	Median	2.86	3.65	4.21	4.54	4.77	4.66	4.28	3.79	3.31	2.76	2.24	1.98	1.83
	Mean	6.36	6.70	6.88	6.77	6.54	6.15	5.71	5.30	5.05	4.98	5.02	5.22	5.42
	3rd Quartile	8.99	9.34	9.56	9.34	9.10	8.56	8.06	7.72	7.40	7.41	7.53	7.86	8.11
	Maximum	69.48	65.71	68.33	64.76	72.13	60.43	53.66	78.84	103.90	127.03	150.16	173.29	196.42
Entry	Minimum	0	0	0	0	0	0	0	0	0	0	0	0	0
	1st Quartile	0	0	0	0.09	0.13	0.12	0.09	0.02	0	0	0	0	0
	Median	0.19	0.29	0.34	0.38	0.38	0.38	0.33	0.27	0.19	0.13	0.04	0	0
	Mean	0.99	0.97	0.89	0.84	0.81	0.75	0.67	0.60	0.57	0.56	0.58	0.61	0.65
	3rd Quartile	0.81	0.89	0.93	0.92	0.91	0.87	0.79	0.72	0.67	0.62	0.60	0.61	0.64
	Maximum	64.29	66.40	67.40	63.08	70.45	40.92	30.22	11.06	12.71	14.28	15.85	17.42	18.99
Mortality	Minimum	0	0	0	0	0	0	0	0	0	0	0	0	0
	1st Quartile	0	0	0	0	0	0	0	0	0	0	0	0	0
	Median	0	0	0	0.04	0.10	0.09	0.06	0	0	0	0	0	0
	Mean	1.46	1.31	1.17	1.04	0.93	0.84	0.77	0.74	0.74	0.77	0.82	0.87	0.92
	3rd Quartile	0.56	0.62	0.70	0.82	0.87	0.83	0.73	0.57	0.44	0.38	0.35	0.30	0.30
	Maximum	159.91	122.92	85.92	62.07	55.37	48.66	41.95	35.25	28.54	27.41	30.57	33.40	35.90
Harvest	Minimum	0	0	0	0	0	0	0	0	0	0	0	0	0
	1st Quartile	0	0	0	0	0	0	0	0	0	0	0	0	0
	Median	0	0	0	0	0	0	0	0	0	0	0	0	0
	Mean	0.36	1.14	2.11	2.41	2.63	2.96	3.21	3.13	2.86	2.13	1.57	0.87	0.33
	3rd Quartile	0	0	0	0	0	0	0	0	0	0	0	0	0
	Maximum	462.97	469.93	478.33	471.11	474.23	483.09	470.31	573.27	573.37	568.45	574.04	571.40	579.96

Table 1—Distribution Statistics for Population 1

Component	Statistic	1999	2000	2001	2002	2003	2004	2005	2006	2007	2008	2009	2010	2011
								Year						
Volume	Minimum	0	0	0	0	0	0	0	0	0	0	0	0	0
	1st Quartile	4.68	11.1	16.78	21.82	26.3	30.81	34.43	36.86	39.3	40.89	42.37	43.28	44.62
	Median	56.14	64.25	71	76.6	82.02	85.6	88.27	90.41	92.59	95	98.34	102.38	106.3
	Mean	83.06	88.69	94.05	98.69	103.0	106.94	110.14	112.71	114.87	117	119.88	123.33	127.69
	3rd Quartile	127	134.71	141.72	147.24	152.21	156.87	161.05	164.54	167.4	170.31	173.11	178.22	184.87
	Maximum	599.56	602.77	620.56	636.28	650.25	661.39	669.52	674.7	679.09	679.78	676.46	684.32	831.11
Live growth	Minimum	-5.66	-6.86	-43.60	-21.13	-10.62	-13.44	-22.80	-32.27	-24.60	-10.21	-10.94	-6.57	-12.45
	1st Quartile	0	0.46	1.12	1.58	1.95	1.931	1.78	1.29	0.51	0	0	0	0
	Median	2.91	3.72	4.30	4.68	4.96	4.88	4.51	4.02	3.53	2.95	2.408	2.13	1.99
	Mean	6.49	6.84	7.06	6.99	6.79	6.44	6.02	5.61	5.37	5.32	5.36	5.56	5.76
	3rd Quartile	9.10	9.50	9.80	9.63	9.45	8.95	8.49	8.18	7.89	7.91	8.06	8.42	8.67
	Maximum	70.95	67.54	70.22	66.27	74.08	63.73	56.33	83.58	110.91	134.04	157.17	180.30	203.43
Entry	Minimum	0	0	0	0	0	0	0	0	0	0	0	0	0
	1st Quartile	0	0	0	0.09	0.13	0.12	0.10	0.02	0	0	0	0	0
	Median	0.19	0.29	0.35	0.39	0.40	0.39	0.35	0.28	0.20	0.13	0.043	0	0
	Mean	0.99	0.98	0.90	0.86	0.84	0.78	0.71	0.63	0.60	0.60	0.62	0.65	0.69
	3rd Quartile	0.82	0.90	0.95	0.95	0.94	0.91	0.84	0.76	0.71	0.67	0.64	0.65	0.68
	Maximum	65.92	67.49	69.45	43.39	73.56	33.3	32.30	11.83	13.74	15.31	16.88	18.44	20.01
Mortality	Minimum	0	0	0	0	0	0	0	0	0	0	0	0	0
	1st Quartile	0	0	0	0	0	0	0	0	0	0	0	0	0
	Median	0	0	0	0.04	0.11	0.10	0.06	0	0	0	0	0	0
	Mean	1.48	1.33	1.19	1.07	0.97	0.88	0.82	0.78	0.79	0.82	0.87	0.92	0.97
	3rd Quartile	0.56	0.63	0.72	0.84	0.90	0.87	0.77	0.61	0.47	0.40	0.37	0.32	0.31
	Maximum	162.27	125.27	88.28	63.89	57.18	50.48	43.77	37.07	30.36	29.23	32.39	34.55	37.63
Harvest	Minimum	0	0	0	0	0	0	0	0	0	0	0	0	0
	1st Quartile	0	0	0	0	0	0	0	0	0	0	0	0	0
	Median	0	0	0	0	0	0	0	0	0	0	0	0	0
	Mean	0.37	1.14	2.132	2.47	2.73	3.14	3.34	3.3	3.06	2.23	1.66	0.93	0.35
	3rd Quartile	0	0	0	0	0	0	0	0	0	0	0	0	0
	Maximum	461.93	493.15	478.92	486.63	493.17	495.13	497.93	575.7	591.30	590.59	602.60	589.36	628.30

Table 2—Distribution Statistics for Population 2

Component	Statistic	1999	2000	2001	2002	2003	2004	2005	2006	2007	2008	2009	2010	2011
								Year						
Volume	Minimum	0	0	0	0	0	0	0	0	0	0	0	0	0
	1st Quartile	4.68	11.13	16.78	21.74	26.16	30.62	34.15	36.32	38.42	39.84	41.33	42.10	43.36
	Median	56.13	64.25	71.04	76.52	81.91	85.37	87.90	89.73	91.90	94.25	97.37	101.10	104.79
	Mean	83.07	88.72	94.05	98.63	102.91	106.77	109.87	112.23	114.24	116.25	119.01	122.40	126.71
	3rd Quartile	126.99	134.77	141.73	147.21	152.17	156.79	160.95	164.30	167.08	169.98	172.70	177.70	184.12
	Maximum	595.09	603.74	622.28	638.03	651.04	661.42	668.94	673.73	677.89	678.48	675.11	691.20	828.74
Live growth	Minimum	-5.71	-6.83	-43.71	-21.18	-10.77	-13.48	-22.79	-32.38	-24.33	-10.20	-11.00	-6.54	-12.55
	1st Quartile	0	0.46	1.12	1.58	1.95	1.93	1.78	1.29	0.50	0	0	0	0
	Median	2.91	3.71	4.30	4.68	4.96	4.88	4.51	4.02	3.52	2.95	2.41	2.13	1.99
	Mean	6.49	6.84	7.06	6.99	6.79	6.44	6.02	5.61	5.37	5.32	5.36	5.56	5.76
	3rd Quartile	9.10	9.49	9.80	9.63	9.45	8.96	8.49	8.18	7.88	7.91	8.06	8.42	8.67
	Maximum	71.19	67.80	70.52	67.14	74.87	63.18	56.71	83.66	111.09	134.23	157.36	180.49	203.62
Entry	Minimum	0	0	0	0	0	0	0	0	0	0	0	0	0
	1st Quartile	0	0	0	0.09	0.13	0.12	0.10	0.02	0	0	0	0	0
	Median	0.19	0.29	0.35	0.39	0.40	0.39	0.35	0.28	0.20	0.13	0.04	0	0
	Mean	1.00	0.98	0.90	0.86	0.84	0.78	0.71	0.63	0.60	0.60	0.62	0.65	0.69
	3rd Quartile	0.82	0.90	0.95	0.95	0.94	0.91	0.84	0.76	0.71	0.67	0.64	0.65	0.68
	Maximum	66.43	67.37	69.43	42.65	73.55	33.63	32.12	11.68	13.49	15.06	16.63	18.20	19.76
Mortality	Minimum	0	0	0	0	0	0	0	0	0	0	0	0	0
	1st Quartile	0	0	0	0	0	0	0	0	0	0	0	0	0
	Median	0	0	0	0.04	0.11	0.10	0.06	0	0	0	0	0	0
	Mean	1.48	1.33	1.19	1.07	0.97	0.87	0.82	0.78	0.79	0.82	0.87	0.92	0.97
	3rd Quartile	0.56	0.63	0.72	0.84	0.90	0.87	0.76	0.61	0.47	0.40	0.37	0.32	0.31
	Maximum	162.00	125.00	88.01	63.83	57.13	50.42	43.71	37.01	30.30	29.03	32.19	34.57	37.65
Harvest	Minimum	0	0	0	0	0	0	0	0	0	0	0	0	0
	1st Quartile	0	0	0	0	0	0	0	0	0	0	0	0	0
	Median	0	0	0	0	0	0	0	0	0	0	0	0	0
	Mean	0.34	1.17	2.19	2.51	2.81	3.23	3.55	3.45	3.18	2.35	1.72	0.99	0.38
	3rd Quartile	0	0	0	0	0	0	0	0	0	0	0	0	0
	Maximum	459.38	481.46	485.90	497.54	505.01	504.85	514.68	577.39	586.59	589.27	599.83	594.19	676.00

Table 3—Distribution Statistics for Population 3

Component	Statistic	Year												
		1999	2000	2001	2002	2003	2004	2005	2006	2007	2008	2009	2010	2011
Volume	Minimum	0	0	0	0	0	0	0	0	0	0	0	0	0
	1st Quartile	4.95	11.35	16.92	21.96	26.34	30.84	33.85	36.19	38.53	39.87	41.12	42.26	43.58
	Median	56.68	64.91	71.49	76.92	82.19	85.65	86.53	88.33	90.98	93.18	96.48	100.53	103.69
	Mean	84.02	89.49	94.64	99.10	103.25	106.97	108.10	110.65	112.81	114.99	117.83	121.32	125.72
	3rd Quartile	127.27	135.26	142.04	147.53	152.35	156.86	157.92	161.43	164.42	167.13	170.33	175.53	181.97
	Maximum	667.96	609.09	628.10	644.38	658.01	668.73	667.17	672.10	676.24	676.75	673.31	688.97	822.51
Live growth	Minimum	-5.68	-6.76	-43.76	-21.12	-10.72	-13.35	-22.78	-32.17	-24.85	-10.08	-11.08	-6.56	-12.57
	1st Quartile	0	0.47	1.12	1.58	1.95	1.93	1.78	1.29	0.50	0	0	0	0
	Median	2.93	3.73	4.31	4.68	4.96	4.88	4.51	4.02	3.52	2.95	2.41	2.13	1.99
	Mean	6.53	6.85	7.06	6.99	6.79	6.44	6.02	5.61	5.37	5.32	5.36	5.56	5.76
	3rd Quartile	9.16	9.51	9.80	9.63	9.45	8.95	8.49	8.18	7.88	7.91	8.06	8.42	8.67
	Maximum	71.03	67.42	70.88	66.71	74.77	63.07	56.87	84.05	111.66	134.79	157.92	181.05	204.18
Entry	Minimum	0	0	0	0	0	0	0	0	0	0	0	0	0
	1st Quartile	0	0	0	0.09	0.13	0.12	0.10	0.02	0	0	0	0	0
	Median	0.19	0.29	0.35	0.39	0.40	0.39	0.35	0.28	0.20	0.13	0.04	0	0
	Mean	0.99	0.99	0.91	0.86	0.84	0.78	0.71	0.63	0.60	0.60	0.62	0.65	0.69
	3rd Quartile	0.82	0.90	0.95	0.95	0.95	0.91	0.84	0.76	0.71	0.67	0.64	0.65	0.68
	Maximum	66.93	67.97	69.15	43.37	72.30	44.83	32.57	11.77	13.61	15.17	16.74	18.31	19.88
Mortality	Minimum	0	0	0	0	0	0	0	0	0	0	0	0	0
	1st Quartile	0	0	0	0	0	0	0	0	0	0	0	0	0
	Median	0	0	0	0.04	0.11	0.38	0.06	0	0	0	0	0	0
	Mean	1.68	1.53	1.39	1.27	1.17	2.96	0.81	0.78	0.78	0.81	0.84	0.89	0.94
	3rd Quartile	0.58	0.65	0.75	0.87	0.97	3.13	0.76	0.60	0.46	0.40	0.36	0.32	0.30
	Maximum	161.99	132.67	124.81	116.96	109.11	101.25	43.73	37.02	30.31	28.49	31.57	34.65	37.73
Harvest	Minimum	0	0	0	0	0	0	0	0	0	0	0	0	0
	1st Quartile	0	0	0	0	0	0	0	0	0	0	0	0	0
	Median	0	0	0	0	0	0	0	0	0	0	0	0	0
	Mean	0.37	1.16	2.11	2.43	2.74	3.13	3.36	3.31	3.02	2.27	1.65	0.91	0.37
	3rd Quartile	0	0	0	0	0	0	0	0	0	0	0	0	0
	Maximum	455.44	477.77	483.53	484.98	489.37	501.90	506.03	581.44	578.92	584.22	582.56	601.94	628.32

Table 4—Distribution Statistics for Population 4

Component	Statistic	Year												
		1999	2000	2001	2002	2003	2004	2005	2006	2007	2008	2009	2010	2011
Volume	Minimum	0	0	0	0	0	0	0	0	0	0	0	0	0
	1st Quartile	7.55	13.69	18.64	21.62	25.20	27.87	30.13	31.57	32.68	33.18	33.70	34.31	35.19
	Median	60.42	67.19	72.32	76.17	79.53	80.75	80.88	80.38	80.30	80.88	81.91	83.56	85.78
	Mean	86.40	91.11	95.22	98.23	100.65	102.47	103.42	103.70	103.65	103.61	104.24	105.51	107.70
	3rd Quartile	130.65	137.25	143.28	146.07	148.62	150.60	151.03	151.21	151.33	151.43	152.03	152.77	155.92
	Maximum	608.21	602.18	615.03	625.44	634.34	640.85	645.19	647.47	649.17	648.63	645.73	640.58	674.22
Live growth	Minimum	-4.73	-5.33	-32.68	-15.17	-7.41	-9.00	-14.86	-20.59	-15.24	-6.27	-6.59	-3.93	-7.37
	1st Quartile	0	0.49	0.92	1.20	1.37	1.33	1.17	0.83	0.31	0	0	0	0
	Median	2.47	3.05	3.31	3.43	3.49	3.33	2.97	2.58	2.22	1.83	1.46	1.28	1.15
	Mean	5.69	5.83	5.64	5.29	4.89	4.44	3.97	3.61	3.39	3.34	3.40	3.59	3.81
	3rd Quartile	7.69	7.87	7.65	7.08	6.71	6.12	5.60	5.25	4.97	4.94	4.99	5.24	5.50
	Maximum	67.08	60.22	60.14	52.60	57.23	45.53	37.36	53.90	69.99	93.12	116.25	139.38	162.51
Entry	Minimum	0	0	0	0	0	0	0	0	0	0	0	0	0
	1st Quartile	0	0	0	0.08	0.11	0.10	0.08	0.01	0	0	0	0	0
	Median	0.19	0.27	0.31	0.33	0.33	0.32	0.28	0.22	0.15	0.10	0.03	0	0
	Mean	0.94	0.84	0.80	0.76	0.70	0.61	0.58	0.50	0.47	0.47	0.49	0.52	0.56
	3rd Quartile	0.78	0.81	0.84	0.81	0.80	0.74	0.67	0.60	0.56	0.52	0.50	0.51	0.54
	Maximum	66.89	62.86	49.51	53.90	24.77	13.09	31.69	9.36	10.71	12.28	13.85	15.41	16.98
Mortality	Minimum	0	0	0	0	0	0	0	0	0	0	0	0	0
	1st Quartile	0	0	0	0	0	0	0	0	0	0	0	0	0
	Median	0	0	0	0.05	0.12	0.11	0.07	0	0	0	0	0	0
	Mean	1.56	1.42	1.28	1.17	1.07	0.99	0.94	0.92	0.93	0.96	1.00	1.03	1.07
	3rd Quartile	0.63	0.70	0.78	0.93	1.01	0.99	0.88	0.71	0.55	0.48	0.44	0.38	0.34
	Maximum	167.89	130.90	93.90	69.67	62.96	56.25	49.55	42.84	36.13	34.56	37.64	40.72	43.80
Harvest	Minimum	0	0	0	0	0	0	0	0	0	0	0	0	0
	1st Quartile	0	0	0	0	0	0	0	0	0	0	0	0	0
	Median	0	0	0	0	0	0	0	0	0	0	0	0	0
	Mean	0.36	1.15	2.14	2.46	2.71	3.11	3.33	3.24	2.97	2.22	1.62	0.89	0.36
	3rd Quartile	0	0	0	0	0	0	0	0	0	0	0	0	0
	Maximum	474.55	479.35	482.29	486.63	485.76	501.16	496.55	542.87	559.86	553.63	552.81	554.08	618.84

Population 0 - Sample Error Structure 1

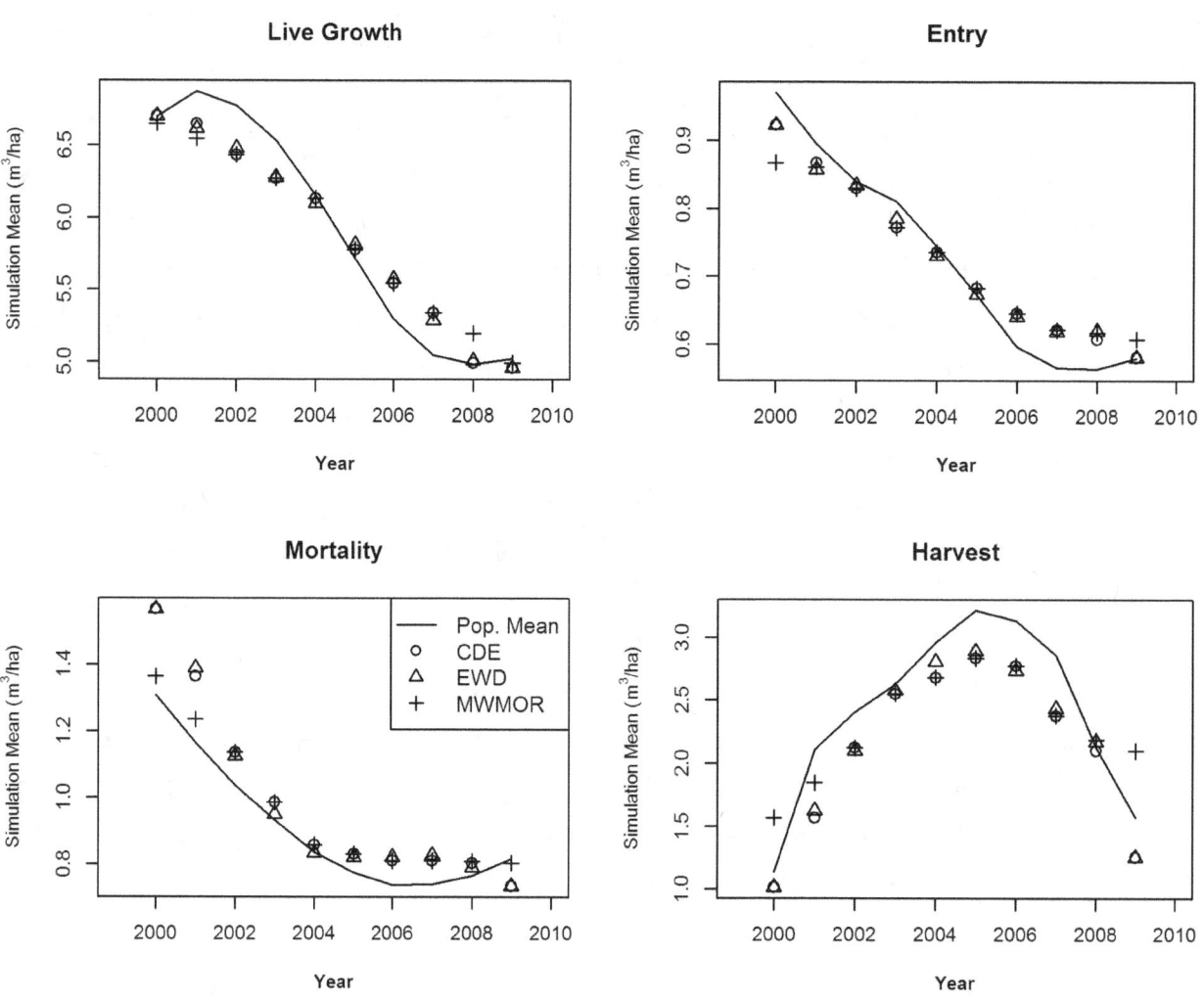

Figure 01M—The mean over 1,000 iterations of 1,000 samples each from Population 0 under Sampling Error Structure 1, for the Centralized Difference Estimator (CDE), the Exponentially Weighted Difference (EWD) estimator, and the Moving-Windows Mean of Ratios (MWMOR) estimator, by growth component and estimation year.

Population 0 - Sample Error Structure 1

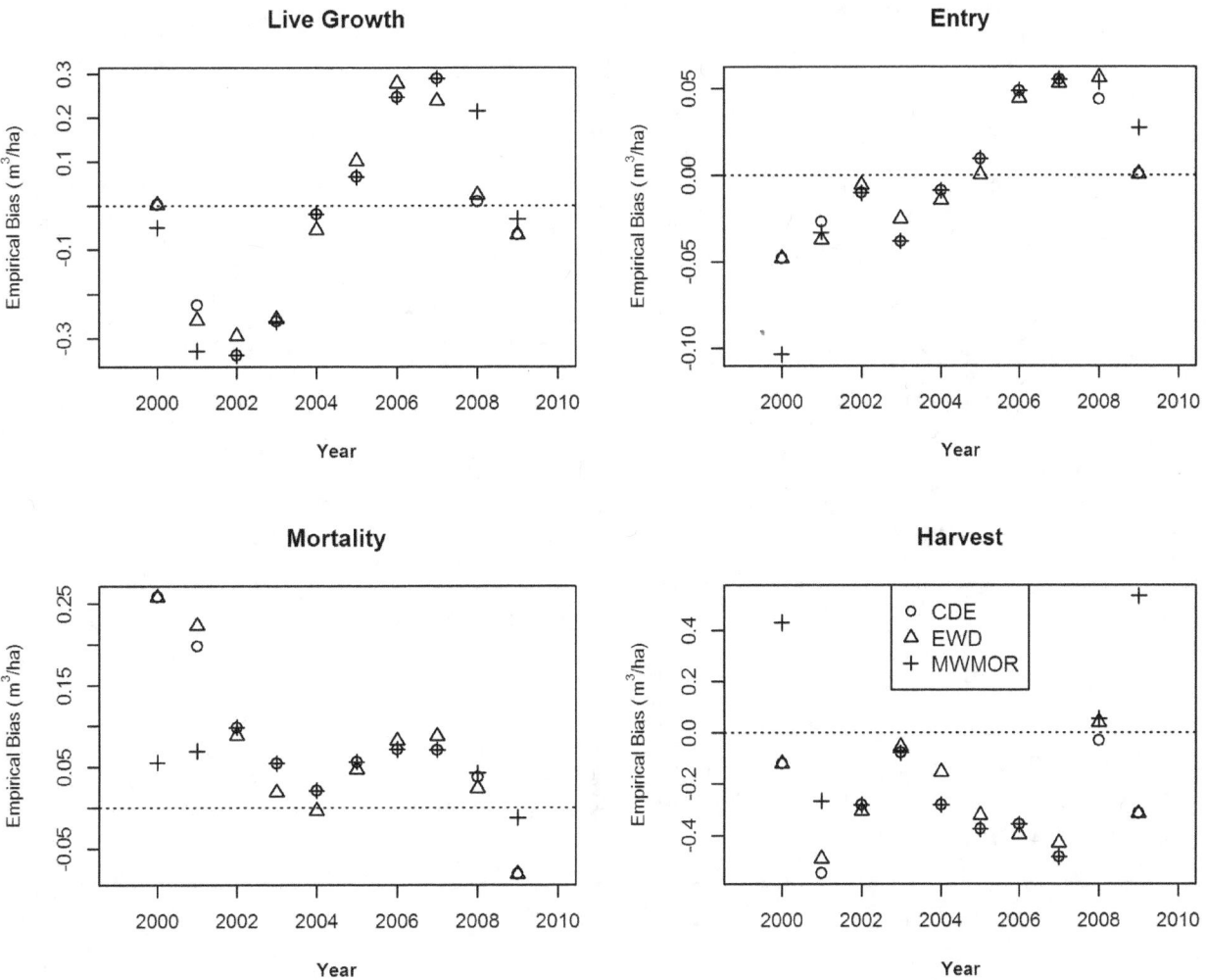

Figure 01B—The empirical bias, over 1,000 iterations of 1,000 samples each from Population 0 under Sampling Error Structure 1, for the Centralized Difference Estimator (CDE), the Exponentially Weighted Difference (EWD) estimator, and the Moving-Windows Mean of Ratios (MWMOR) estimator, by growth component and estimation year.

Population 0 - Sample Error Structure 1

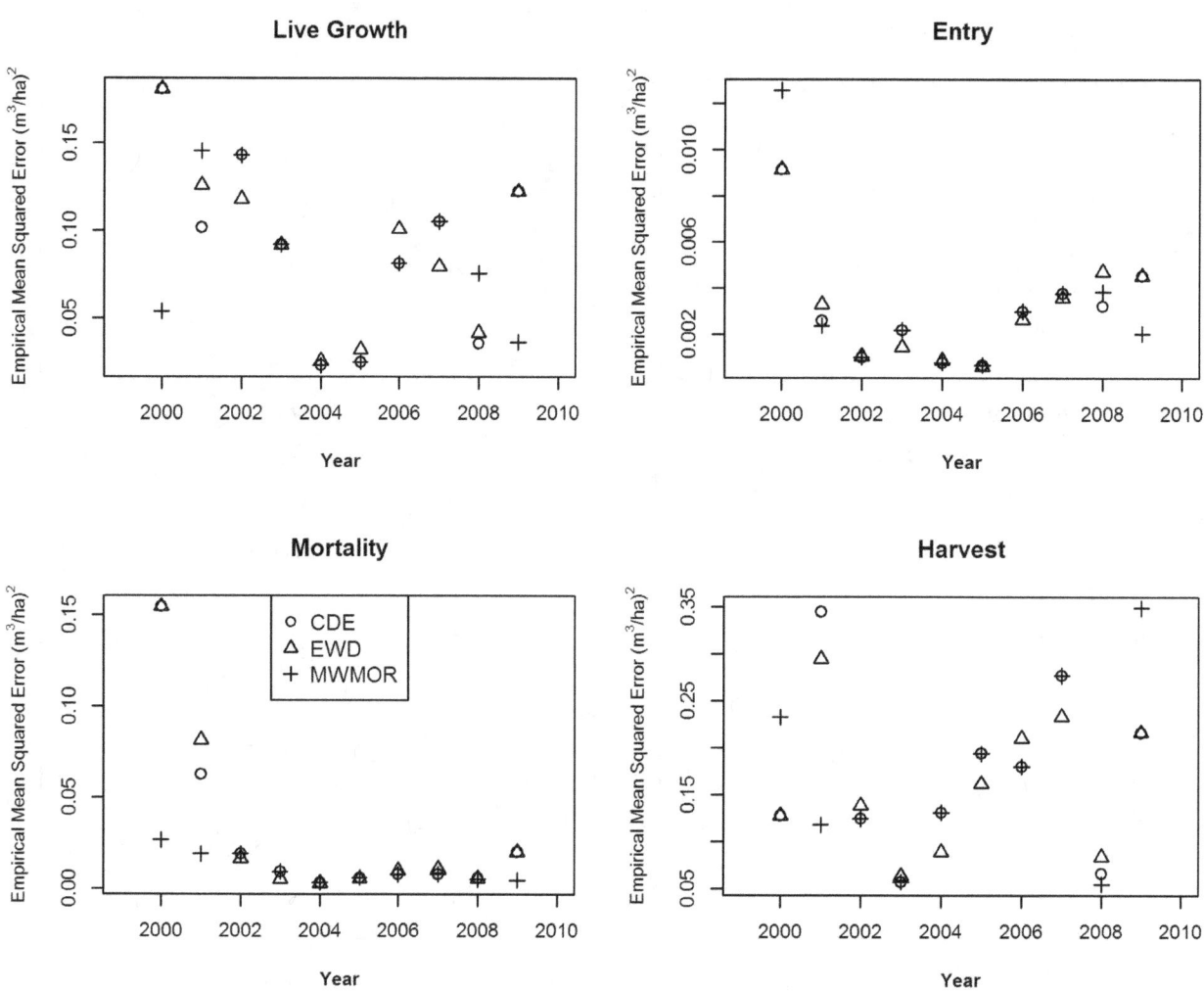

Figure 01E—The empirical mean squared error, over 1,000 iterations of 1,000 samples each from Population 0 under Sampling Error Structure 1, for the Centralized Difference Estimator (CDE), the Exponentially Weighted Difference (EWD) estimator, and the Moving-Windows Mean of Ratios (MWMOR) estimator, by growth component and estimation year.

Population 0 - Sample Error Structure 2

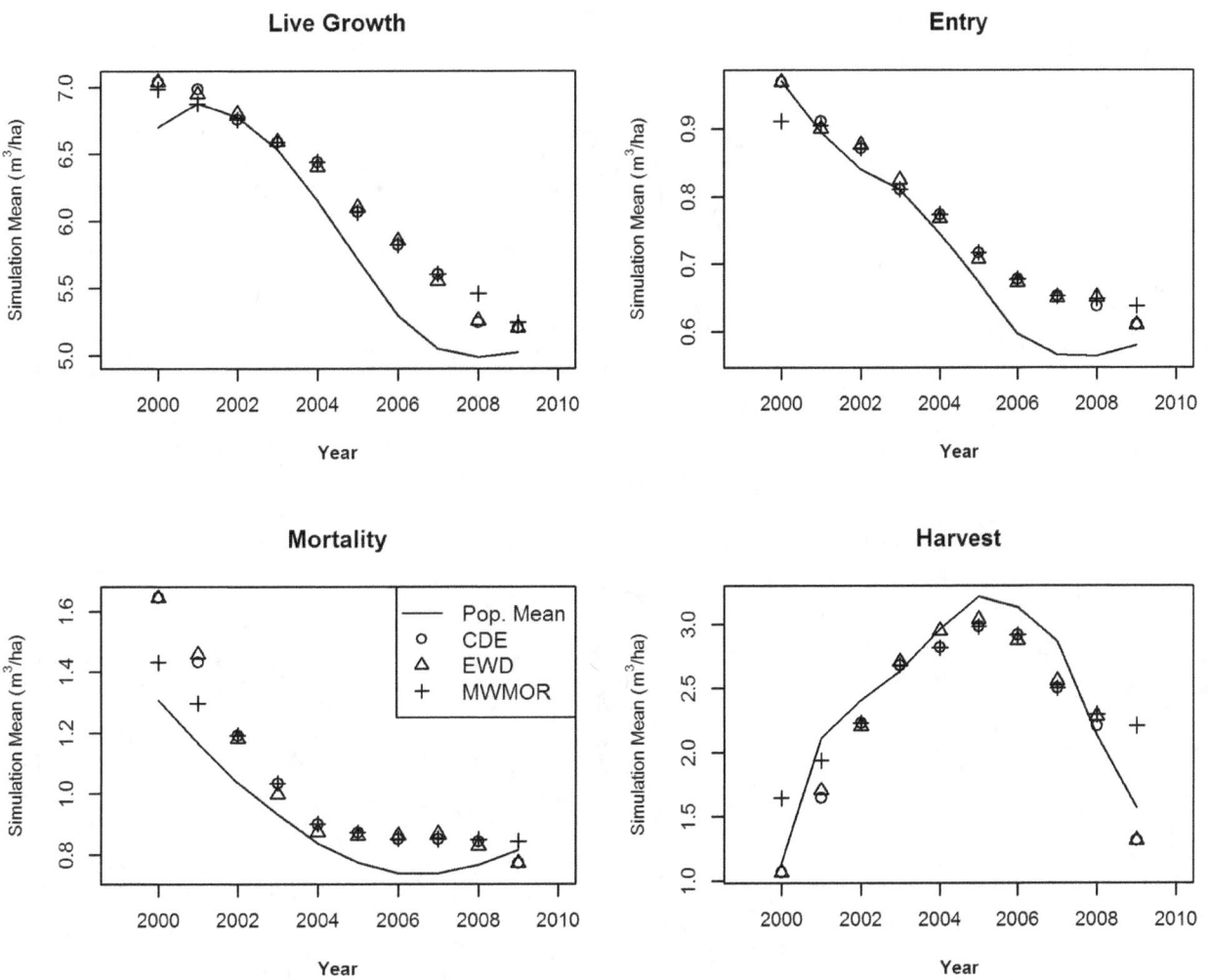

Figure 02M—The mean over 1,000 iterations of 1,000 samples each from Population 0 under Sampling Error Structure 2, for the Centralized Difference Estimator (CDE), the Exponentially Weighted Difference (EWD) estimator, and the Moving-Windows Mean of Ratios (MWMOR) estimator, by growth component and estimation year.

Population 0 - Sample Error Structure 2

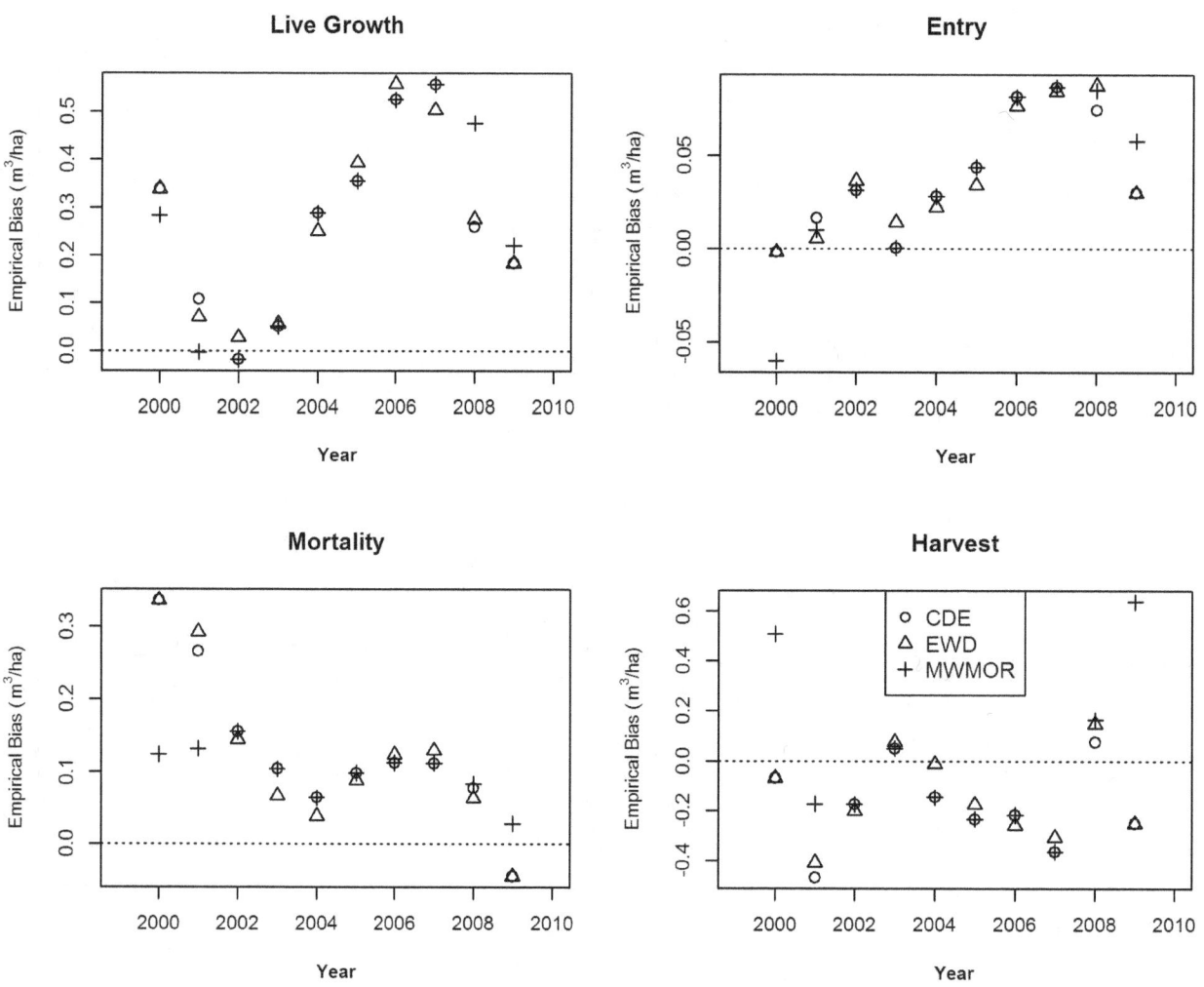

Figure 02B—The empirical bias, over 1,000 iterations of 1,000 samples each from Population 0 under Sampling Error Structure 2, for the Centralized Difference Estimator (CDE), the Exponentially Weighted Difference (EWD) estimator, and the Moving-Windows Mean of Ratios (MWMOR) estimator, by growth component and estimation year.

Population 0 - Sample Error Structure 2

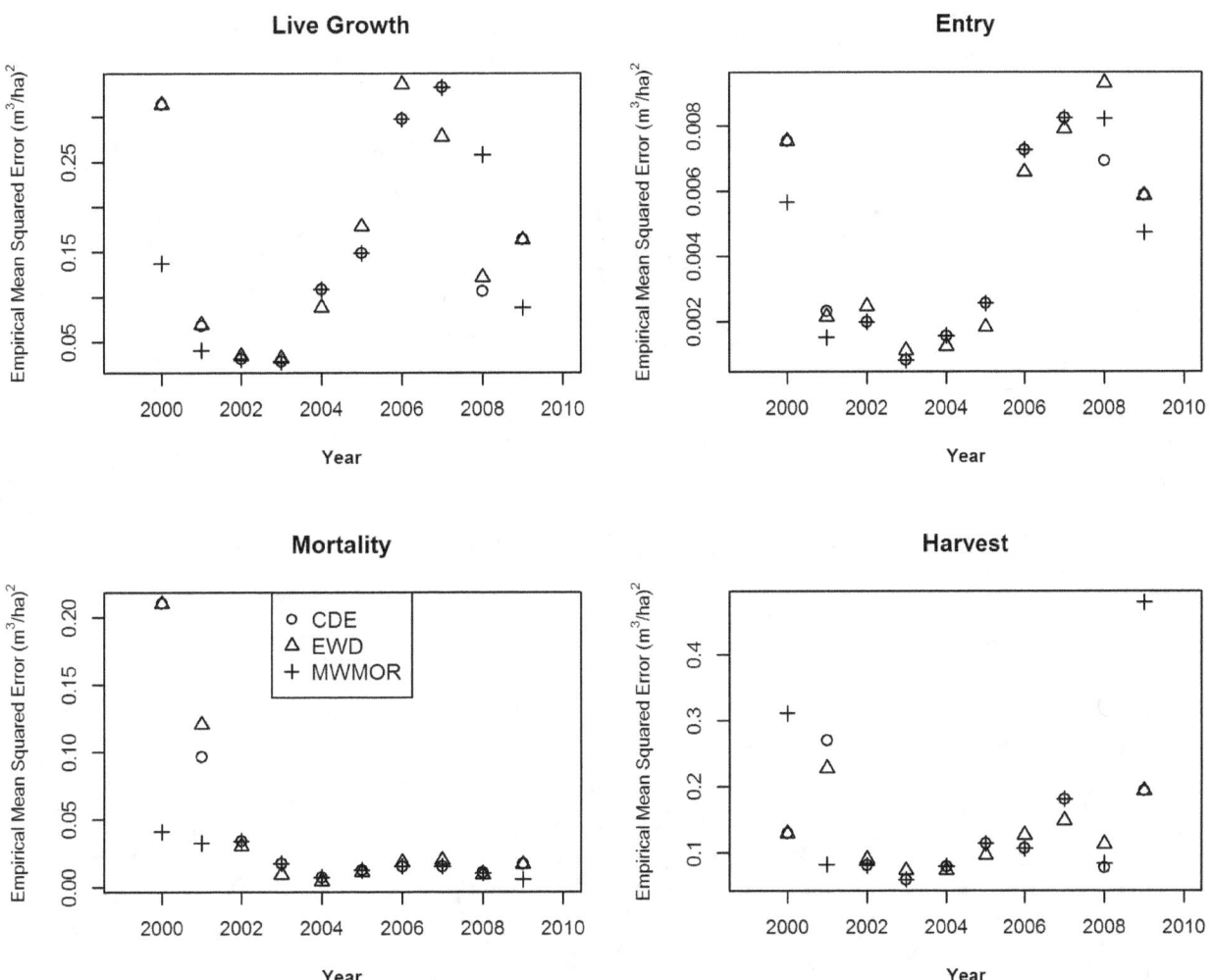

Figure 02E—The empirical mean squared error, over 1,000 iterations of 1,000 samples each from Population 0 under Sampling Error Structure 2, for the Centralized Difference Estimator (CDE), the Exponentially Weighted Difference (EWD) estimator, and the Moving-Windows Mean of Ratios (MWMOR) estimator, by growth component and estimation year.

Population 0 - Sample Error Structure 3

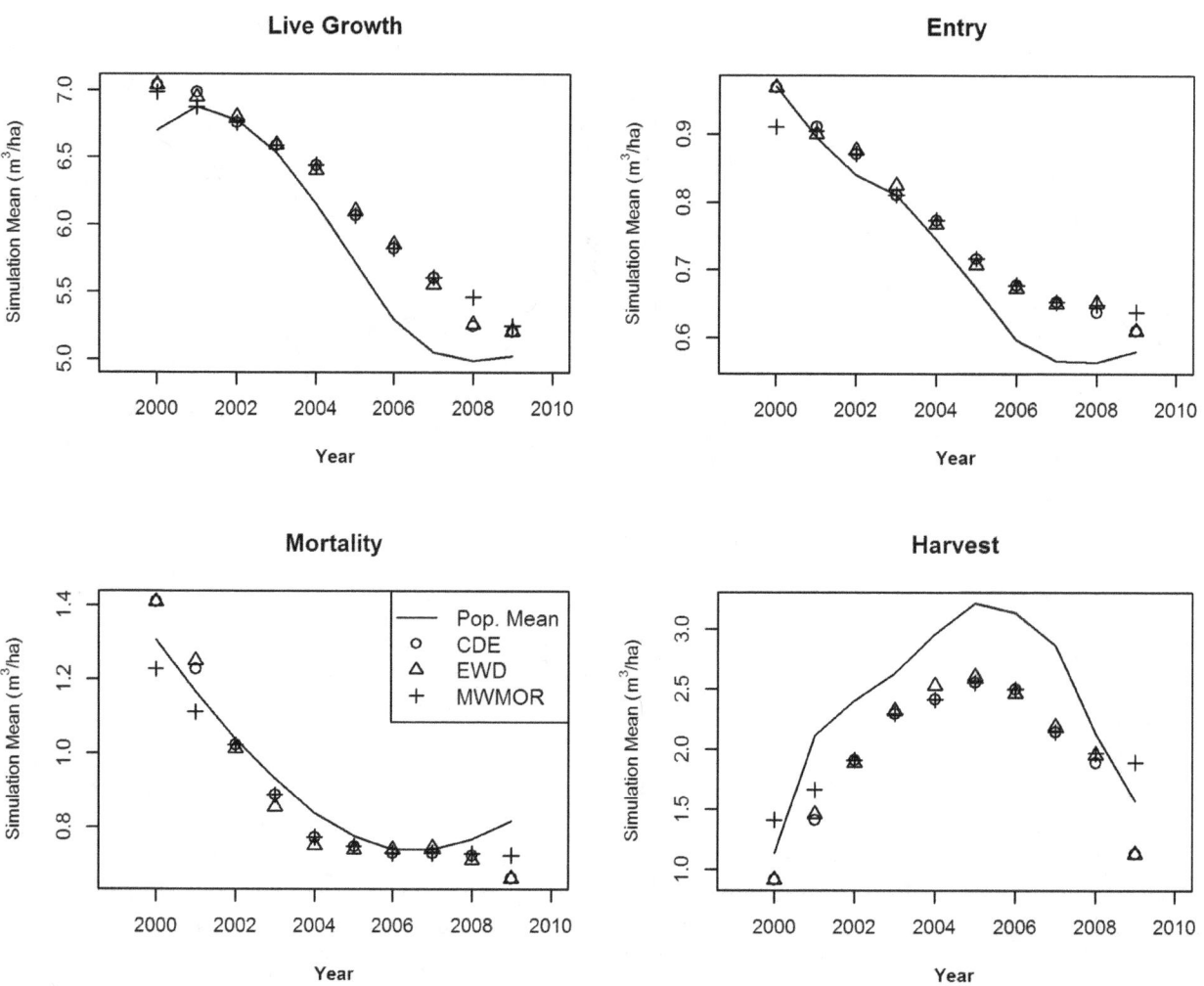

Figure 03M—The mean over 1,000 iterations of 1,000 samples each from Population 0 under Sampling Error Structure 3, for the Centralized Difference Estimator (CDE), the Exponentially Weighted Difference (EWD) estimator, and the Moving-Windows Mean of Ratios (MWMOR) estimator, by growth component and estimation year.

Population 0 - Sample Error Structure 3

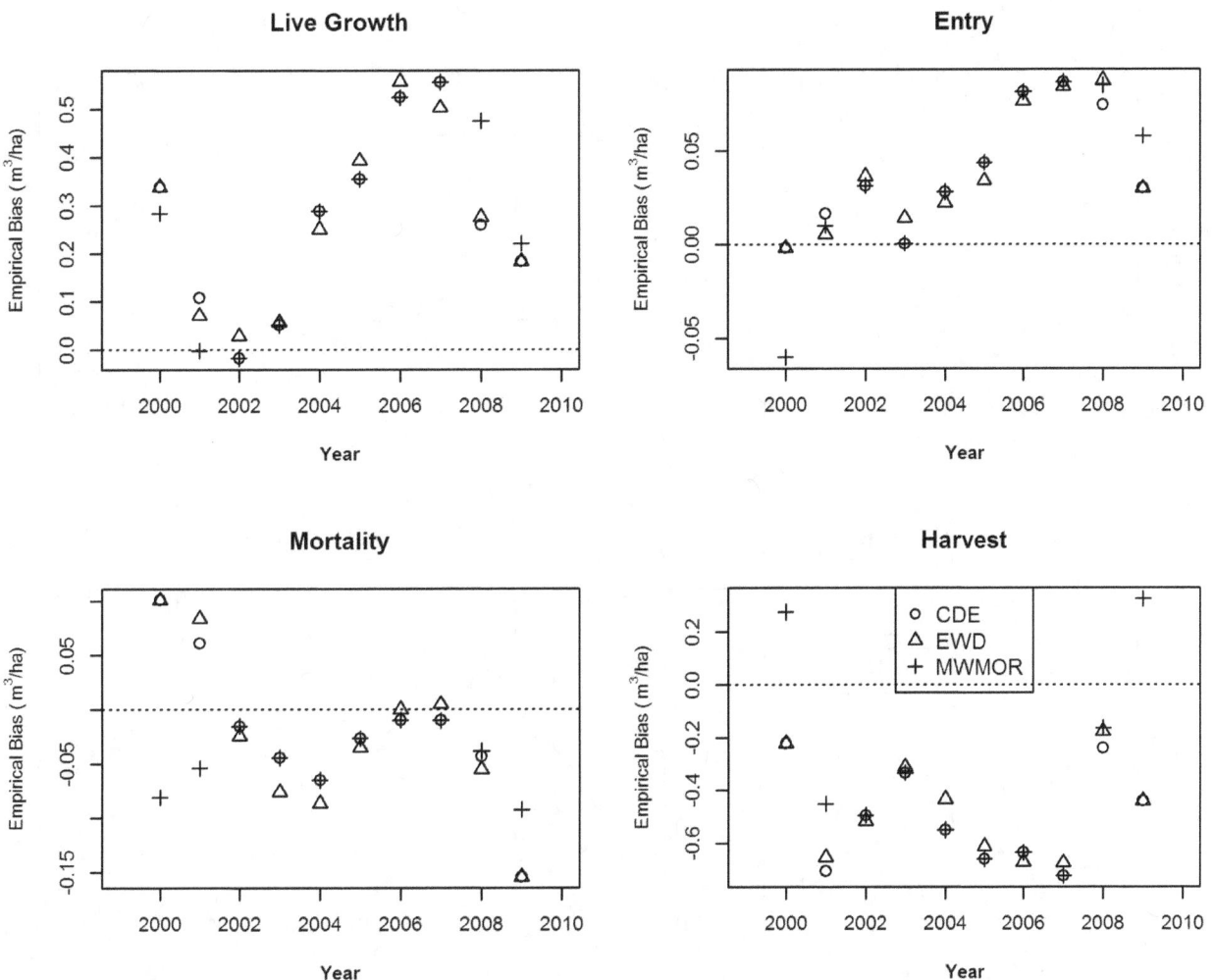

Figure 03B—The empirical bias, over 1,000 iterations of 1,000 samples each from Population 0 under Sampling Error Structure 3, for the Centralized Difference Estimator (CDE), the Exponentially Weighted Difference (EWD) estimator, and the Moving-Windows Mean of Ratios (MWMOR) estimator, by growth component and estimation year.

Population 0 - Sample Error Structure 3

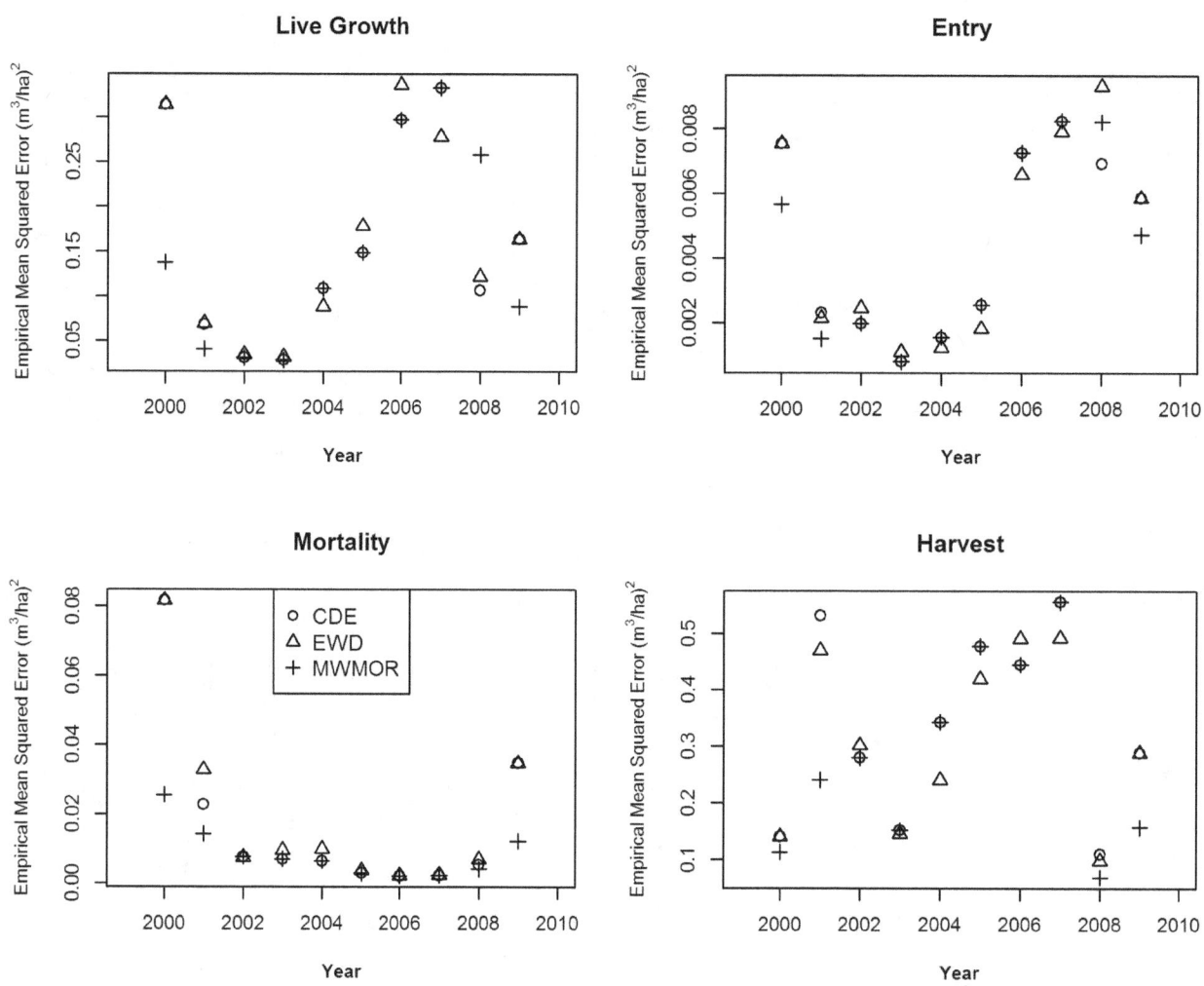

Figure 03E—The empirical mean squared error, over 1,000 iterations of 1,000 samples each from Population 0 under Sampling Error Structure 3, for the Centralized Difference Estimator (CDE), the Exponentially Weighted Difference (EWD) estimator, and the Moving-Windows Mean of Ratios (MWMOR) estimator, by growth component and estimation year.

Population 0 - Sample Error Structure 4

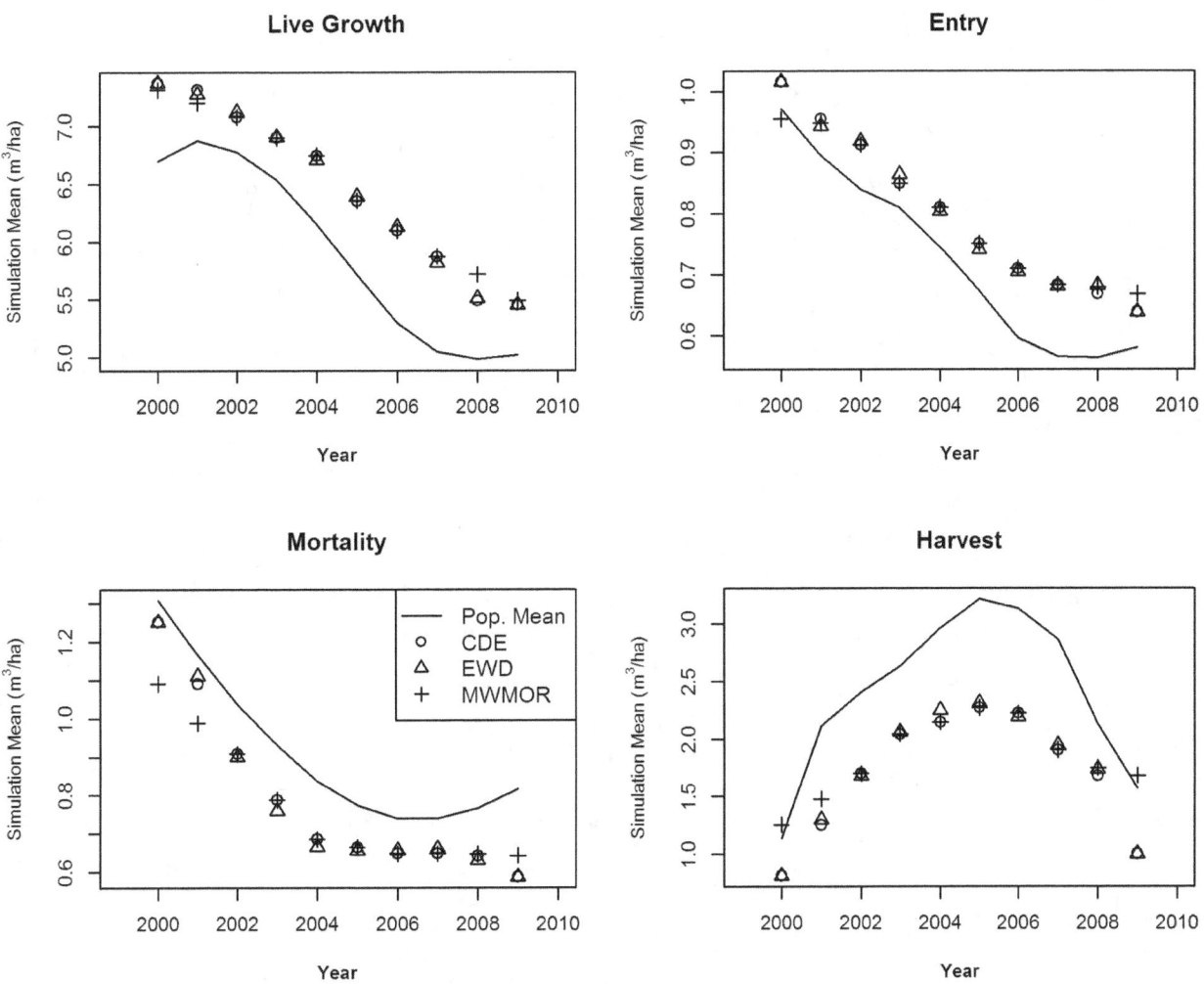

Figure 04M—The mean over 1,000 iterations of 1,000 samples each from Population 0 under Sampling Error Structure 4, for the Centralized Difference Estimator (CDE), the Exponentially Weighted Difference (EWD) estimator, and the Moving-Windows Mean of Ratios (MWMOR) estimator, by growth component and estimation year.

Population 0 - Sample Error Structure 4

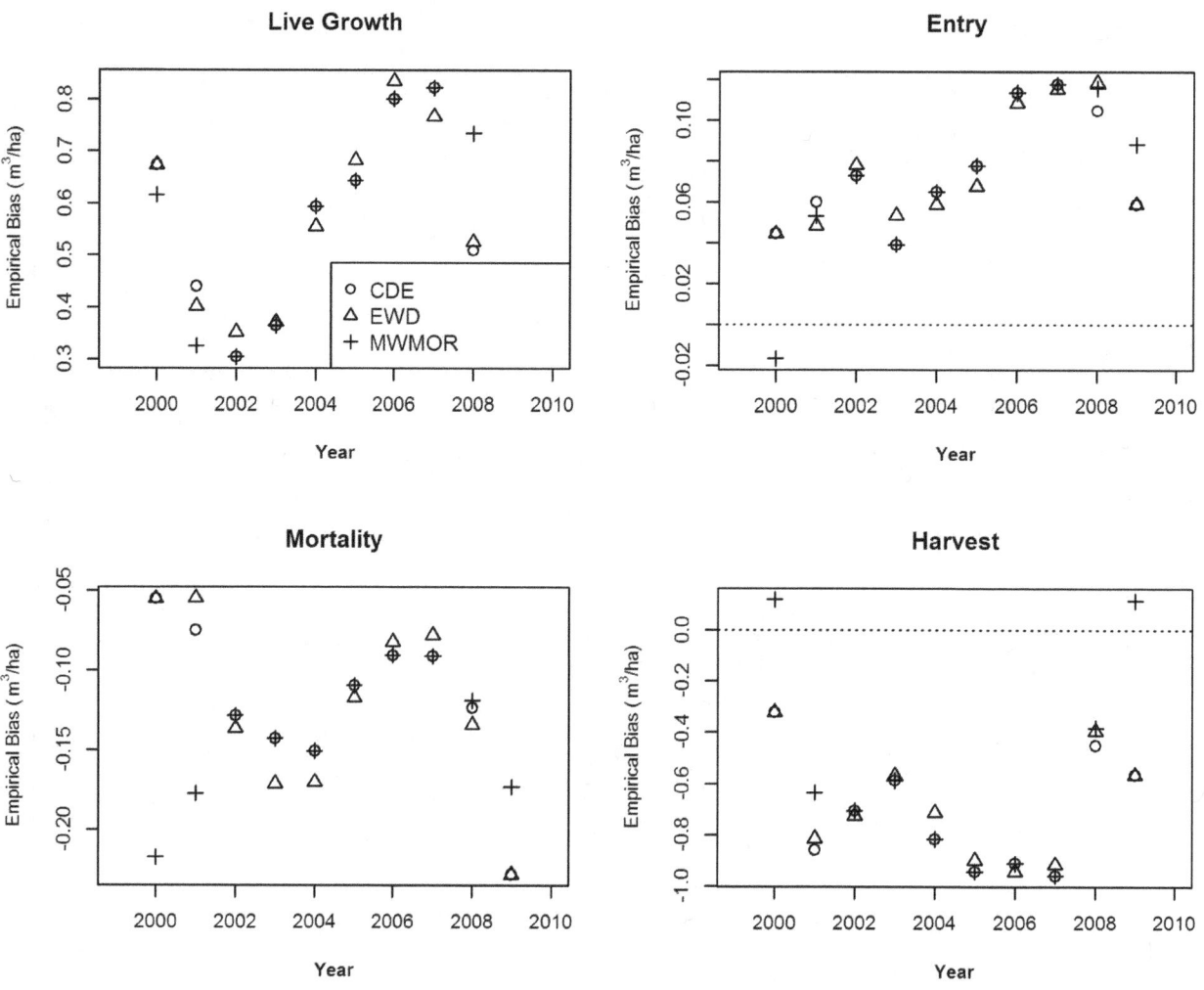

Figure 04B—The empirical bias, over 1,000 iterations of 1,000 samples each from Population 0 under Sampling Error Structure 4, for the Centralized Difference Estimator (CDE), the Exponentially Weighted Difference (EWD) estimator, and the Moving-Windows Mean of Ratios (MWMOR) estimator, by growth component and estimation year.

Population 0 - Sample Error Structure 4

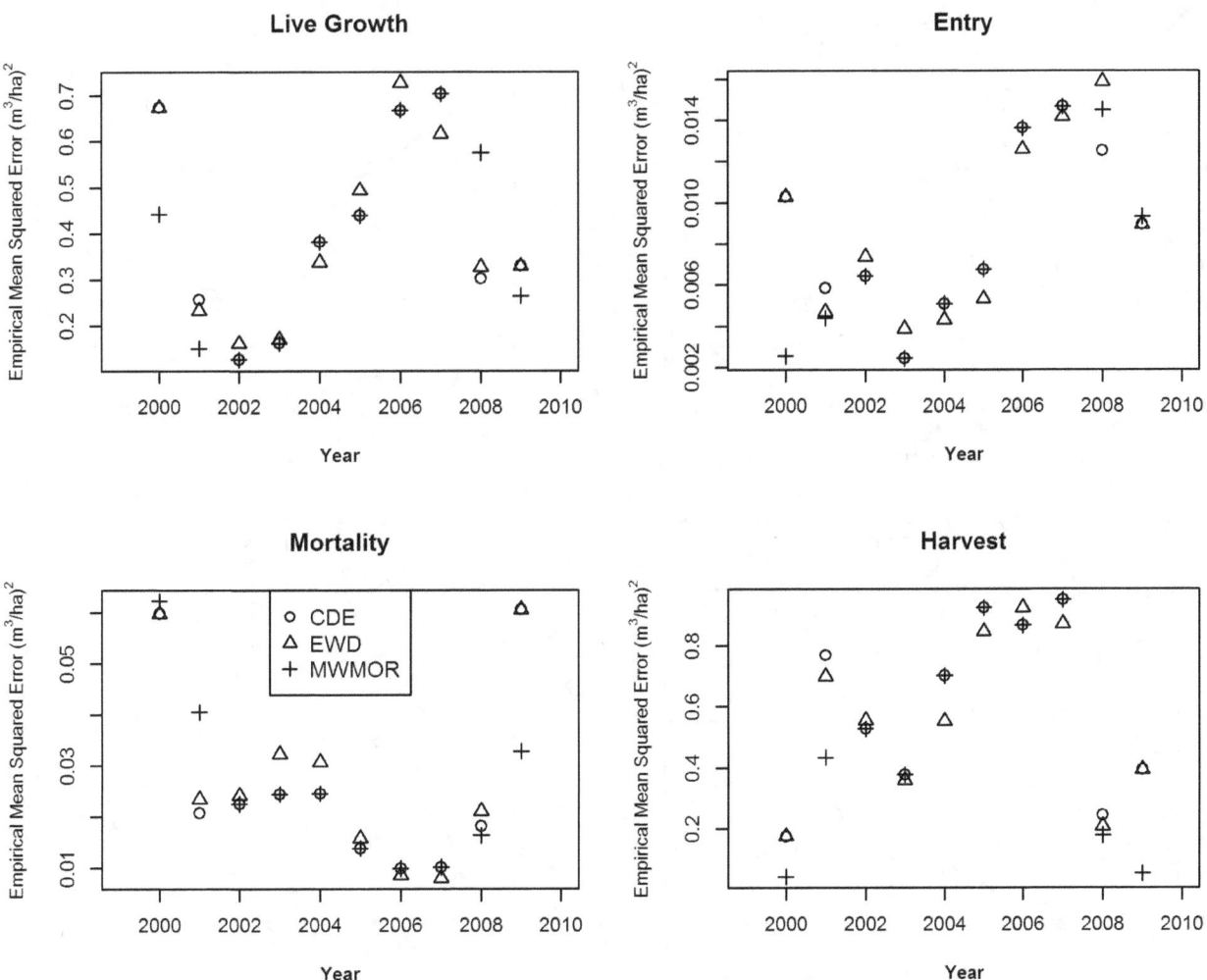

Figure 04E—The empirical mean squared error, over 1,000 iterations of 1,000 samples each from Population 0 under Sampling Error Structure 4, for the Centralized Difference Estimator (CDE), the Exponentially Weighted Difference (EWD) estimator, and the Moving-Windows Mean of Ratios (MWMOR) estimator, by growth component and estimation year.

Population 1 - Sample Error Structure 1

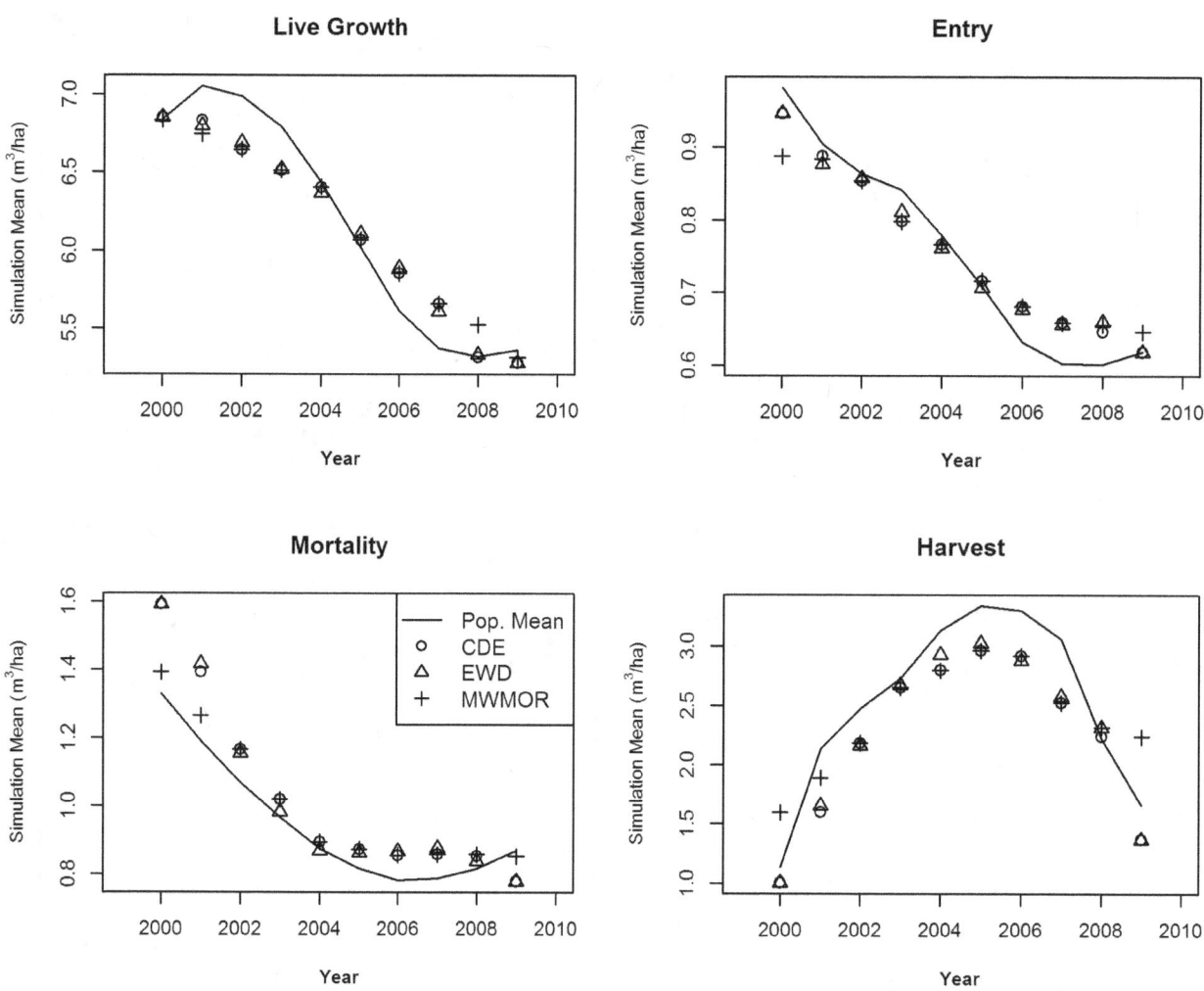

Figure 11M—The mean over 1,000 iterations of 1,000 samples each from Population 1 under Sampling Error Structure 1, for the Centralized Difference Estimator (CDE), the Exponentially Weighted Difference (EWD) estimator, and the Moving-Windows Mean of Ratios (MWMOR) estimator, by growth component and estimation year.

Population 1 - Sample Error Structure 1

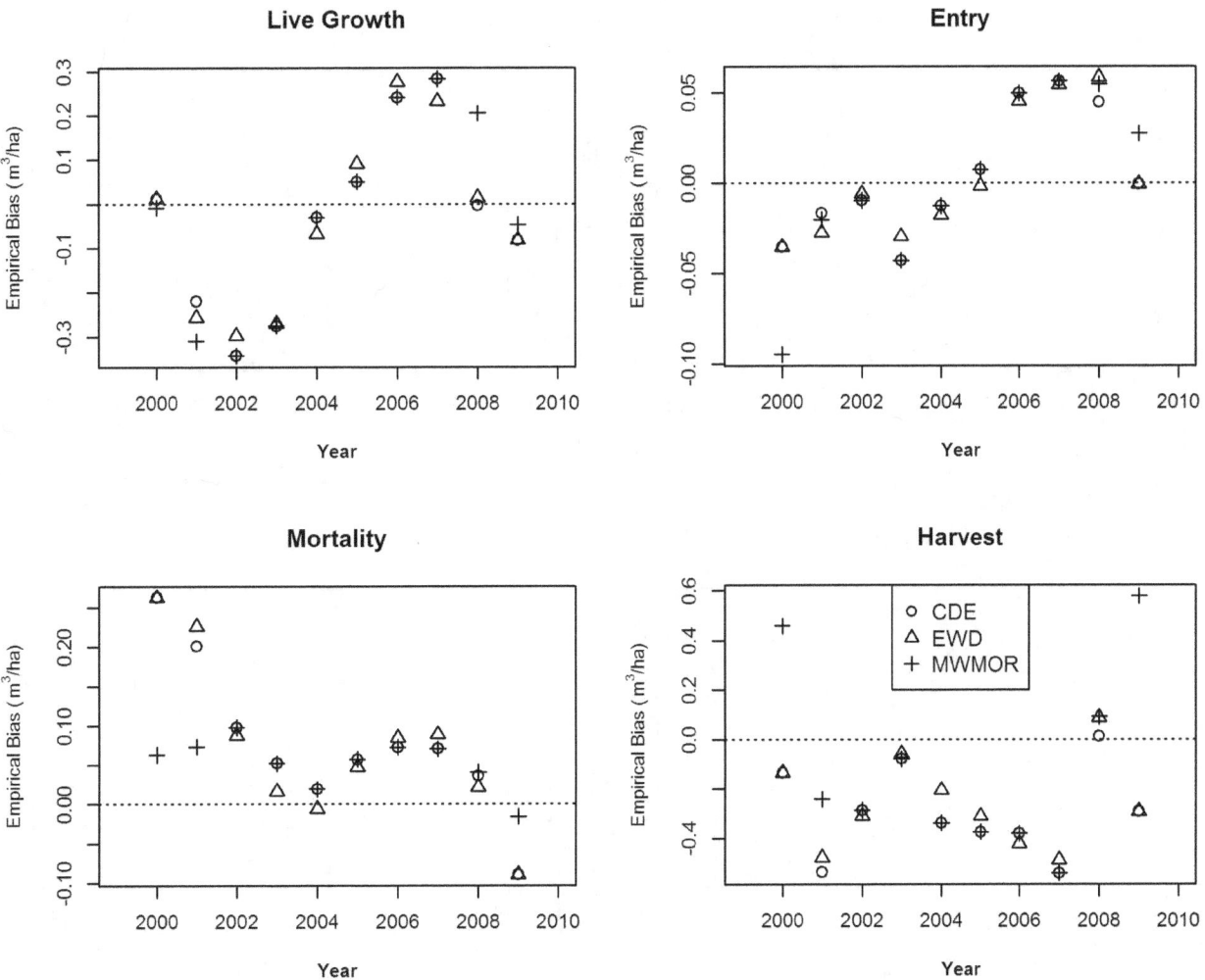

Figure 11B—The empirical bias, over 1,000 iterations of 1,000 samples each from Population 1 under Sampling Error Structure 1, for the Centralized Difference Estimator (CDE), the Exponentially Weighted Difference (EWD) estimator, and the Moving-Windows Mean of Ratios (MWMOR) estimator, by growth component and estimation year.

Population 1 - Sample Error Structure 1

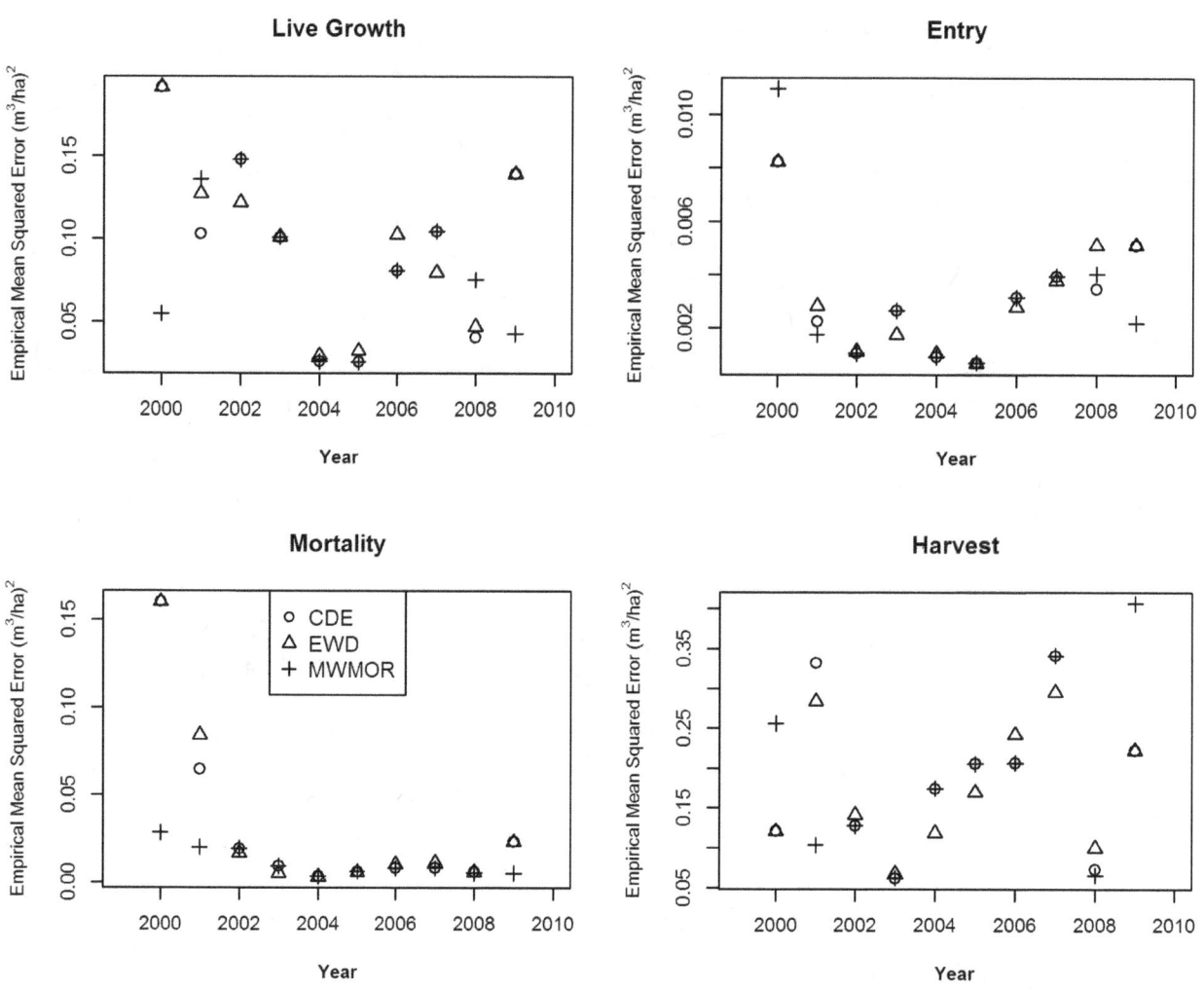

Figure 11E—The empirical mean squared error, over 1,000 iterations of 1,000 samples each from Population 1 under Sampling Error Structure 1, for the Centralized Difference Estimator (CDE), the Exponentially Weighted Difference (EWD) estimator, and the Moving-Windows Mean of Ratios (MWMOR) estimator, by growth component and estimation year.

Population 1 - Sample Error Structure 2

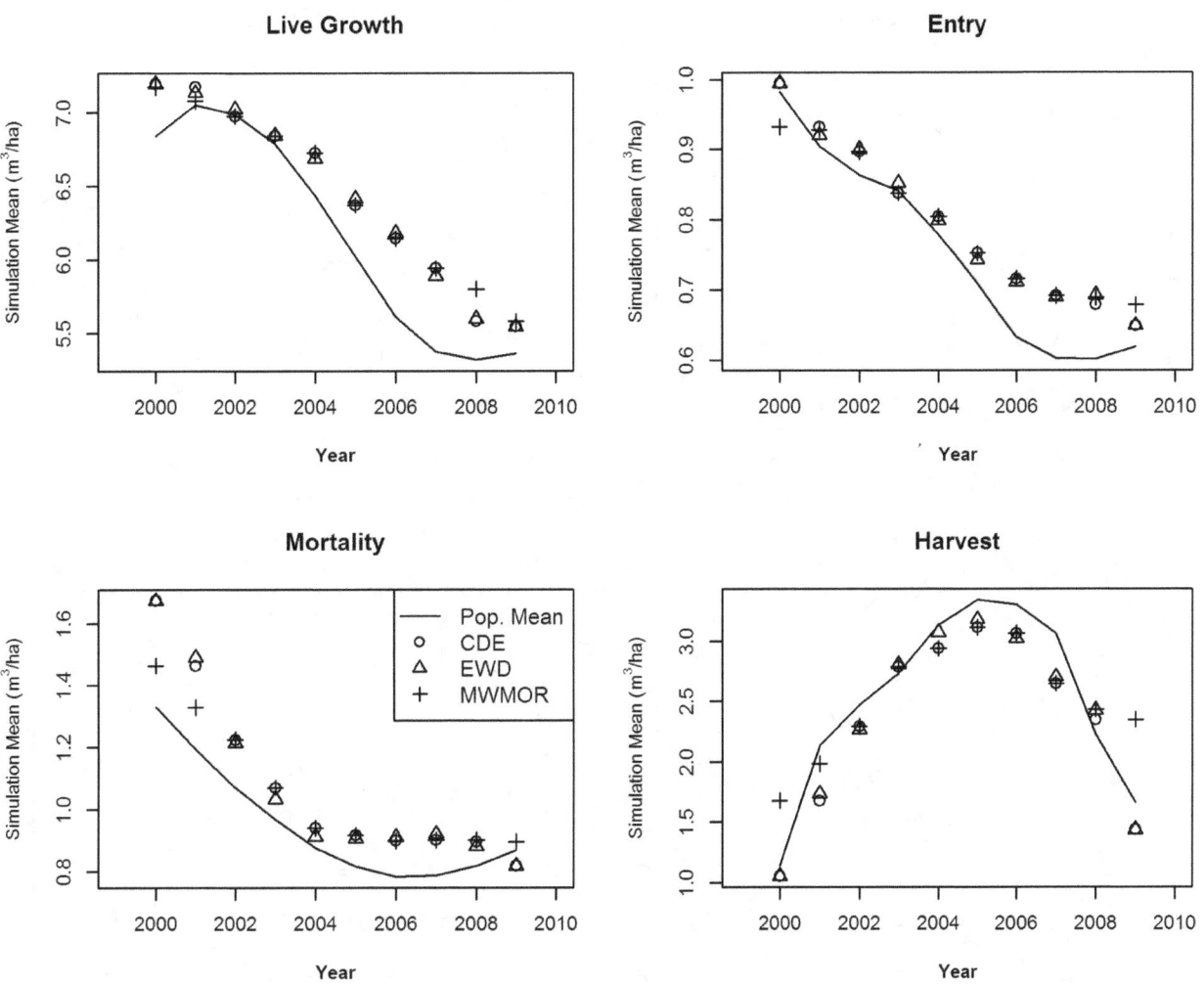

Figure 12M—The mean over 1,000 iterations of 1,000 samples each from Population 1 under Sampling Error Structure 2, for the Centralized Difference Estimator (CDE), the Exponentially Weighted Difference (EWD) estimator, and the Moving-Windows Mean of Ratios (MWMOR) estimator, by growth component and estimation year.

Population 1 - Sample Error Structure 2

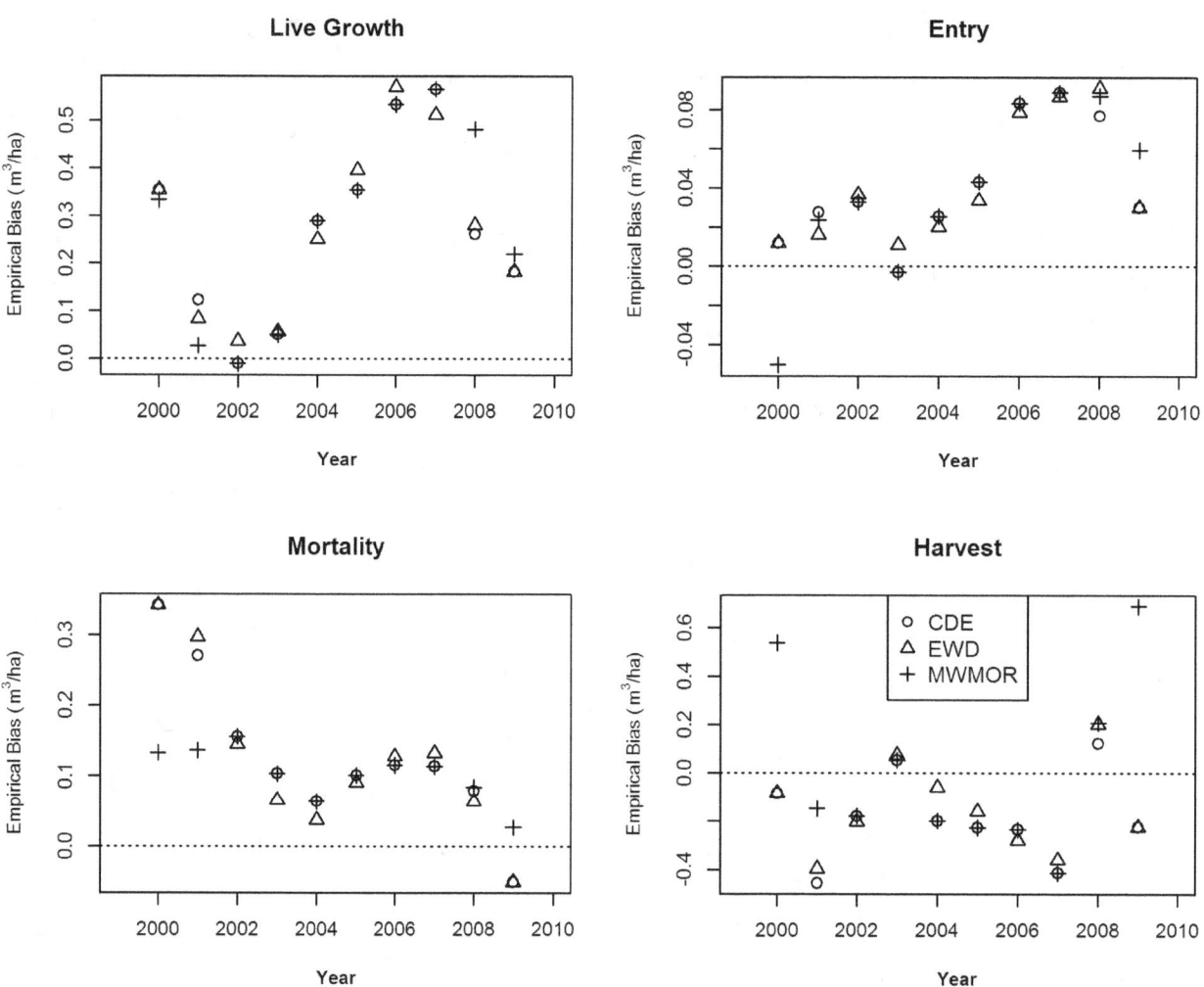

Figure 12B—The empirical bias, over 1,000 iterations of 1,000 samples each from Population 1 under Sampling Error Structure 2, for the Centralized Difference Estimator (CDE), the Exponentially Weighted Difference (EWD) estimator, and the Moving-Windows Mean of Ratios (MWMOR) estimator, by growth component and estimation year.

Population 1 - Sample Error Structure 2

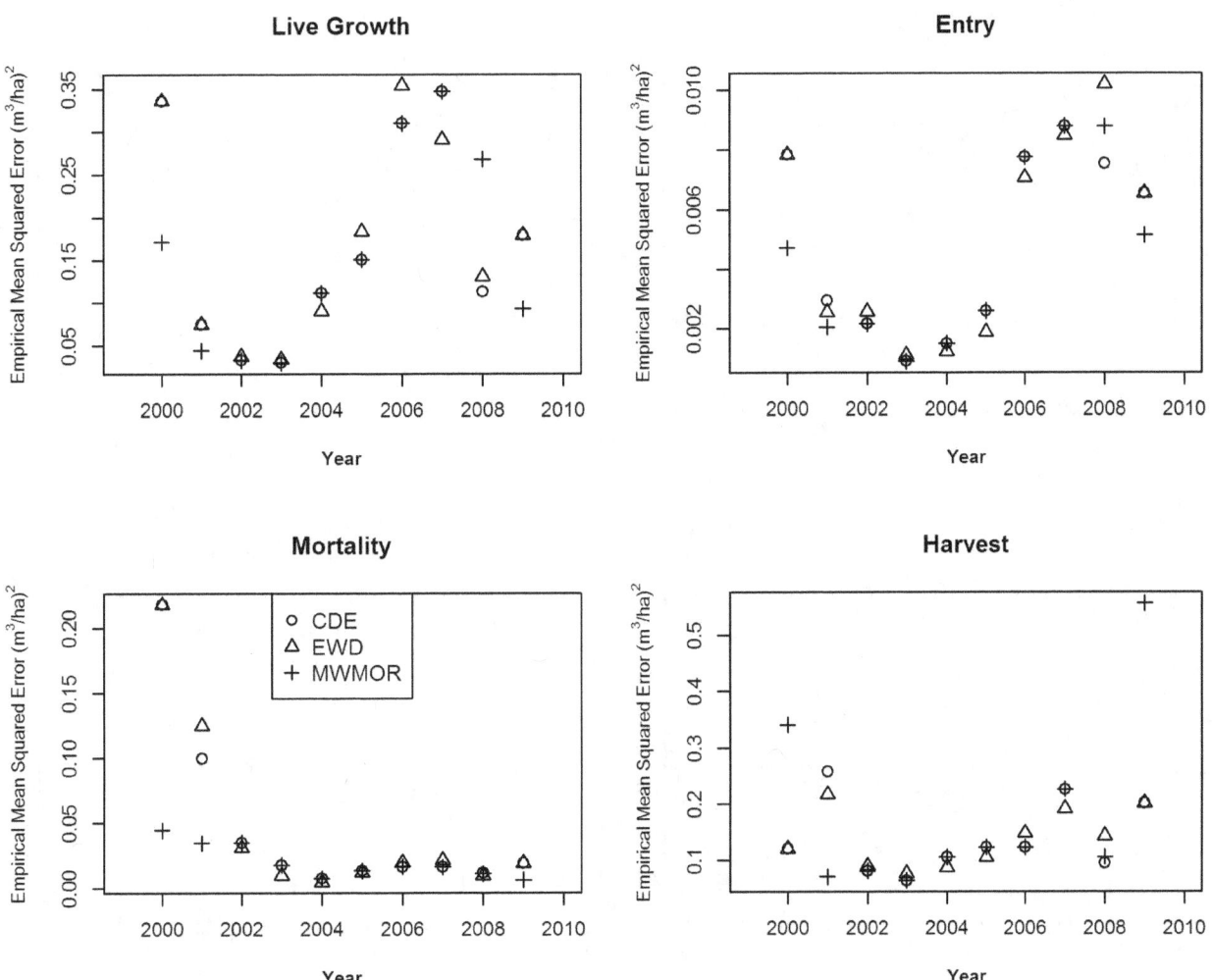

Figure 12E—The empirical mean squared error, over 1,000 iterations of 1,000 samples each from Population 1 under Sampling Error Structure 2, for the Centralized Difference Estimator (CDE), the Exponentially Weighted Difference (EWD) estimator, and the Moving-Windows Mean of Ratios (MWMOR) estimator, by growth component and estimation year.

Population 1 - Sample Error Structure 3

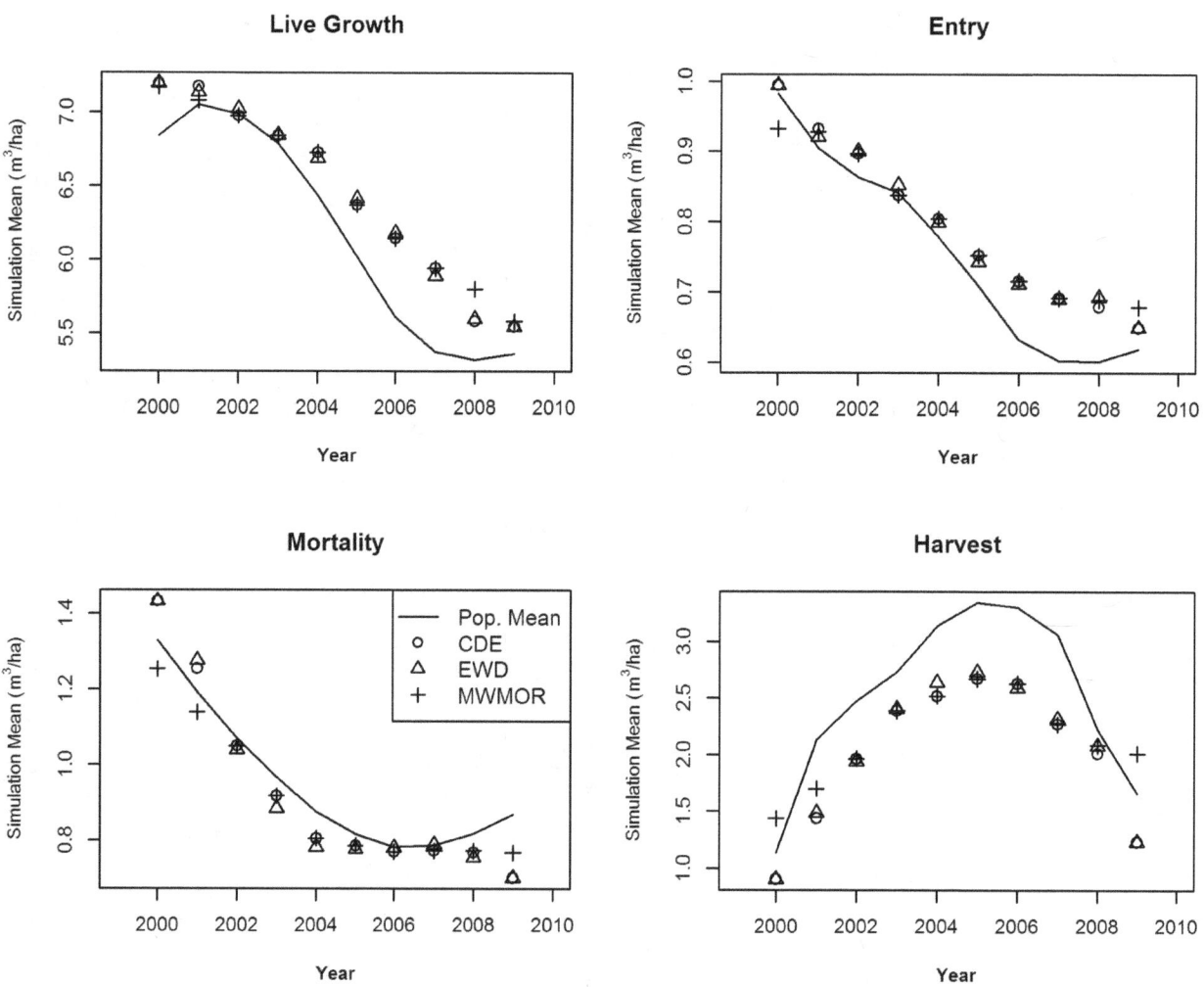

Figure 13M—The mean over 1,000 iterations of 1,000 samples each from Population 1 under Sampling Error Structure 3, for the Centralized Difference Estimator (CDE), the Exponentially Weighted Difference (EWD) estimator, and the Moving-Windows Mean of Ratios (MWMOR) estimator, by growth component and estimation year.

Population 1 - Sample Error Structure 3

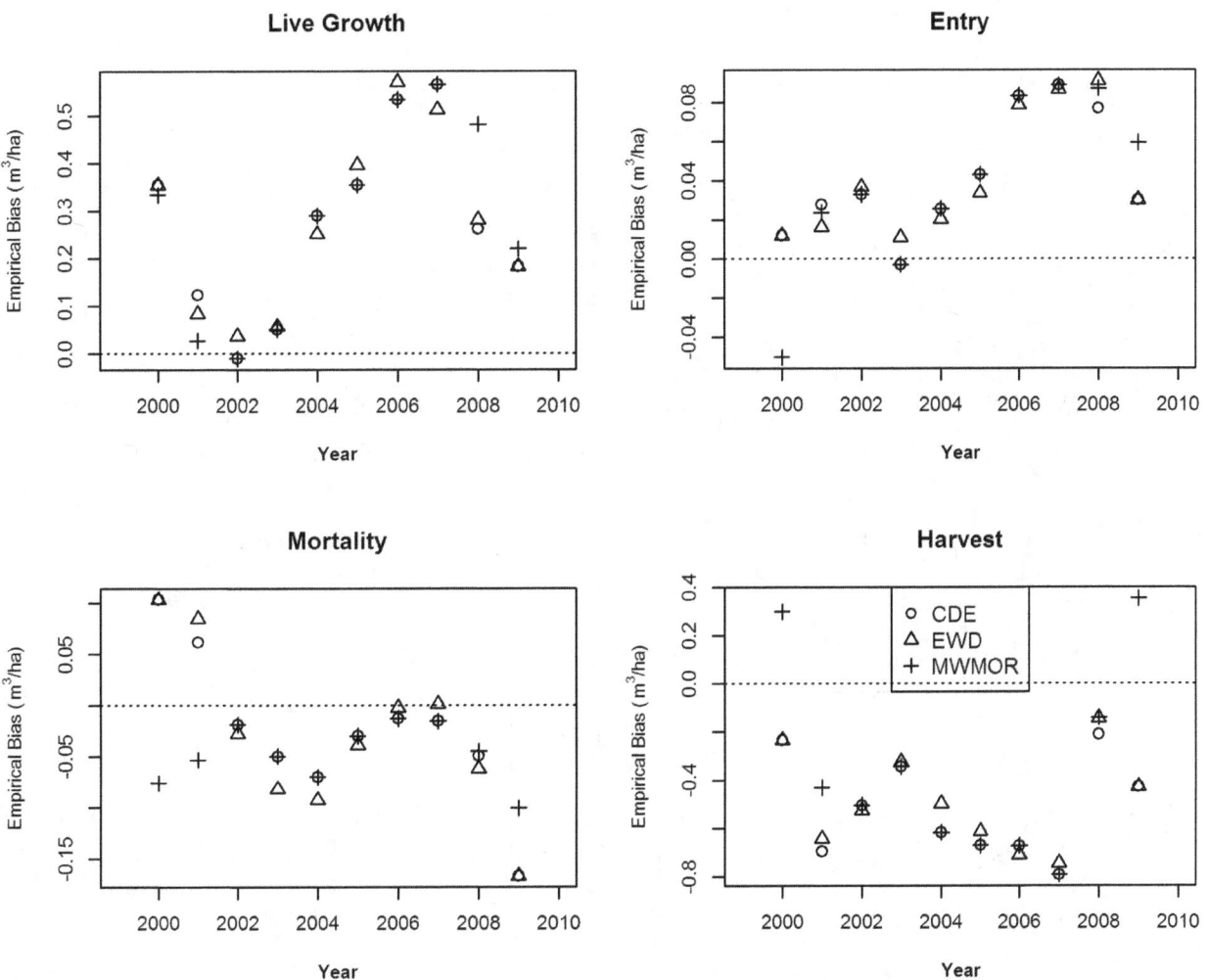

Figure 13B—The empirical bias, over 1,000 iterations of 1,000 samples each from Population 1 under Sampling Error Structure 3, for the Centralized Difference Estimator (CDE), the Exponentially Weighted Difference (EWD) estimator, and the Moving-Windows Mean of Ratios (MWMOR) estimator, by growth component and estimation year.

Population 1 - Sample Error Structure 3

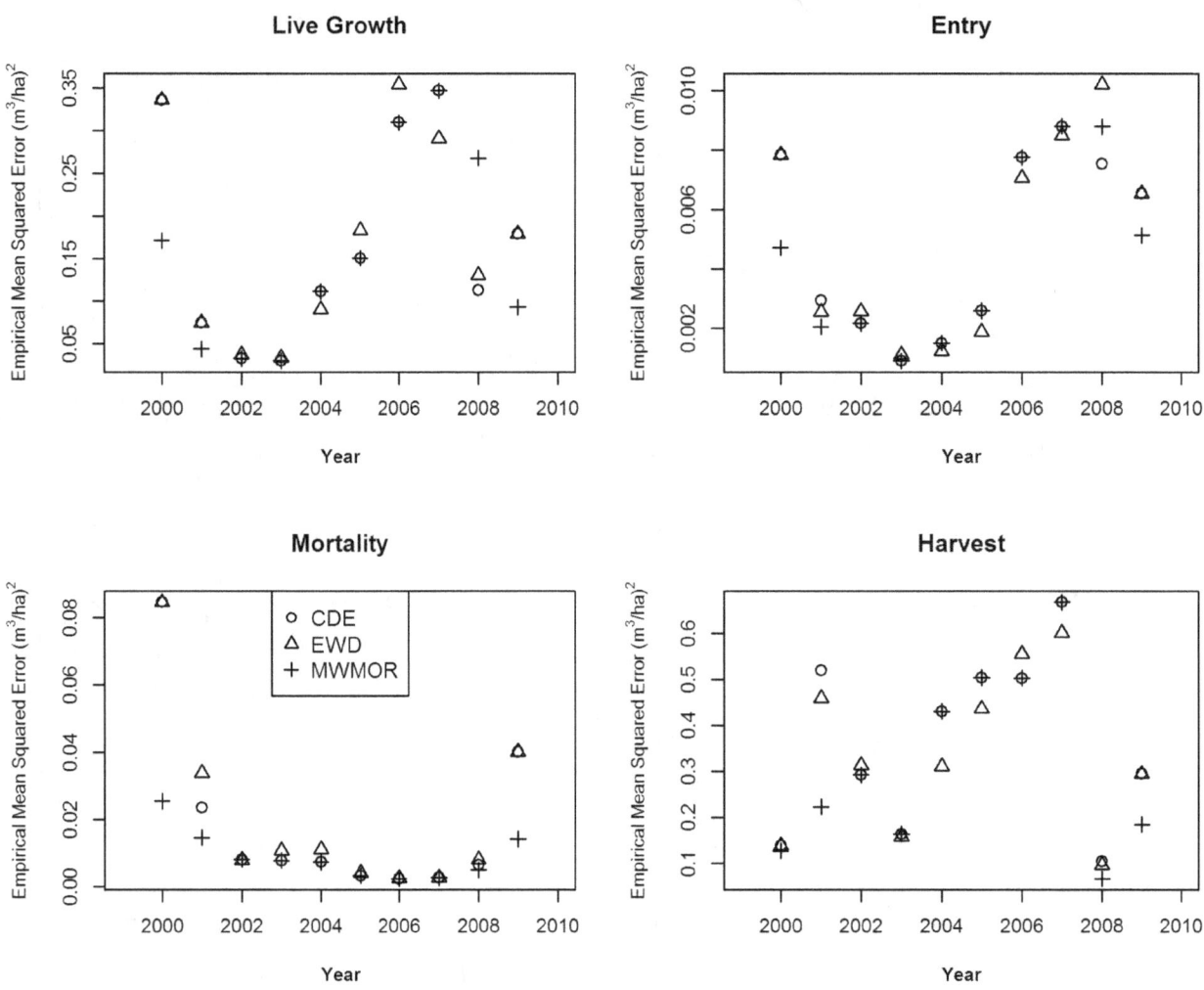

Figure 13E—The empirical mean squared error, over 1,000 iterations of 1,000 samples each from Population 1 under Sampling Error Structure 3, for the Centralized Difference Estimator (CDE), the Exponentially Weighted Difference (EWD) estimator, and the Moving-Windows Mean of Ratios (MWMOR) estimator, by growth component and estimation year.

Population 1 - Sample Error Structure 4

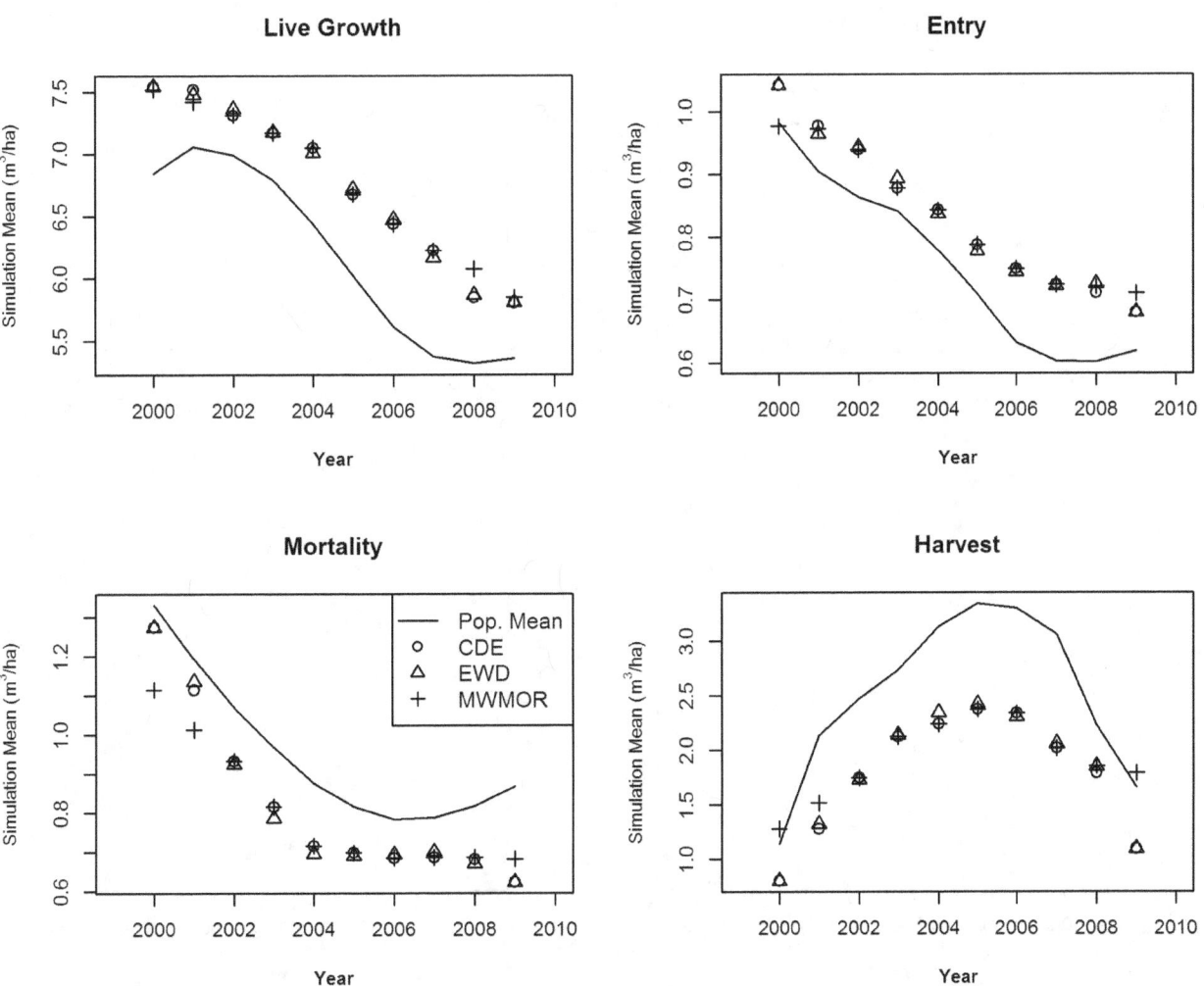

Figure 14M—The mean over 1,000 iterations of 1,000 samples each from Population 1 under Sampling Error Structure 4, for the Centralized Difference Estimator (CDE), the Exponentially Weighted Difference (EWD) estimator, and the Moving-Windows Mean of Ratios (MWMOR) estimator, by growth component and estimation year.

Population 1 - Sample Error Structure 4

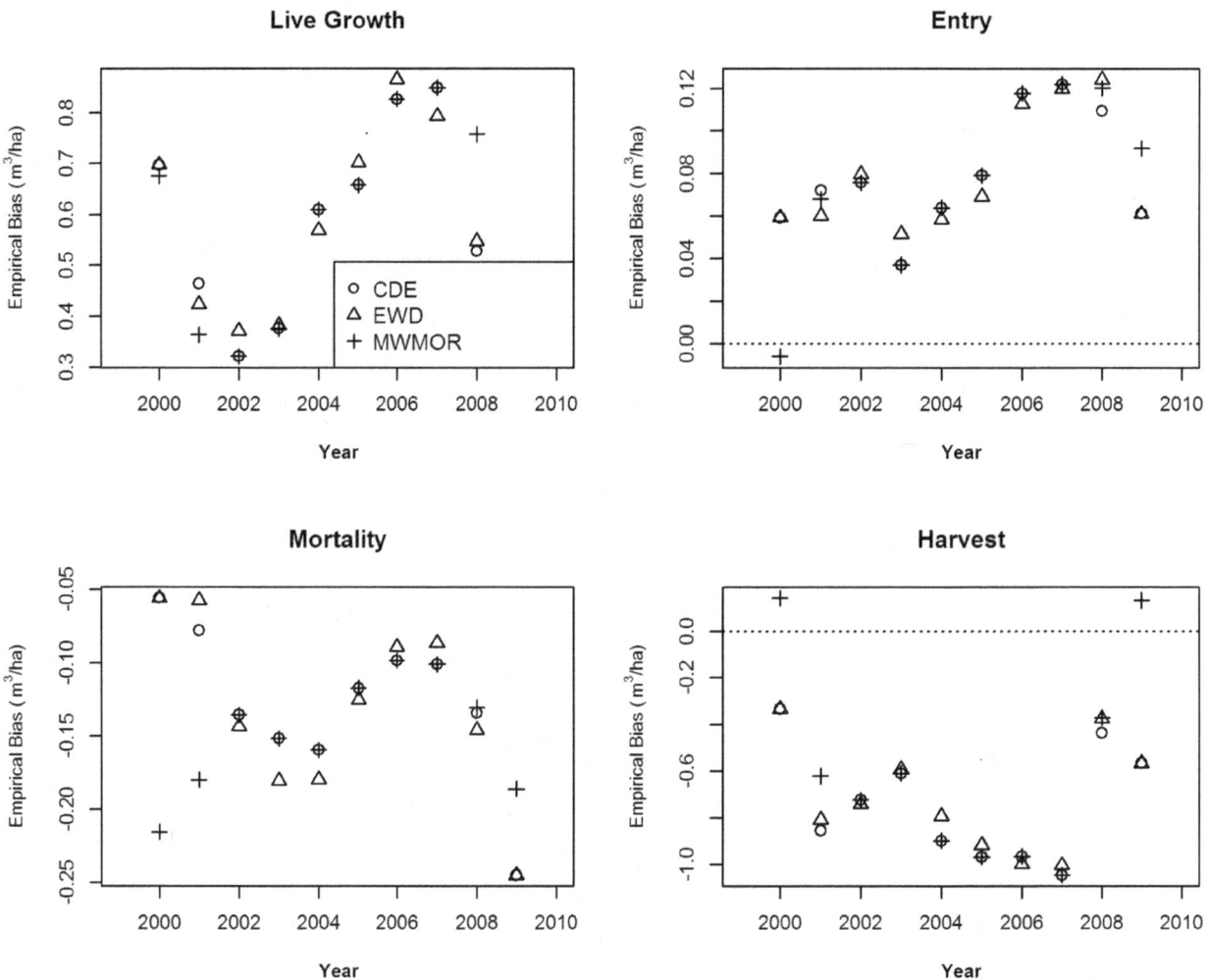

Figure 14B—The empirical bias, over 1,000 iterations of 1,000 samples each from Population 1 under Sampling Error Structure 4, for the Centralized Difference Estimator (CDE), the Exponentially Weighted Difference (EWD) estimator, and the Moving-Windows Mean of Ratios (MWMOR) estimator, by growth component and estimation year.

Population 1 - Sample Error Structure 4

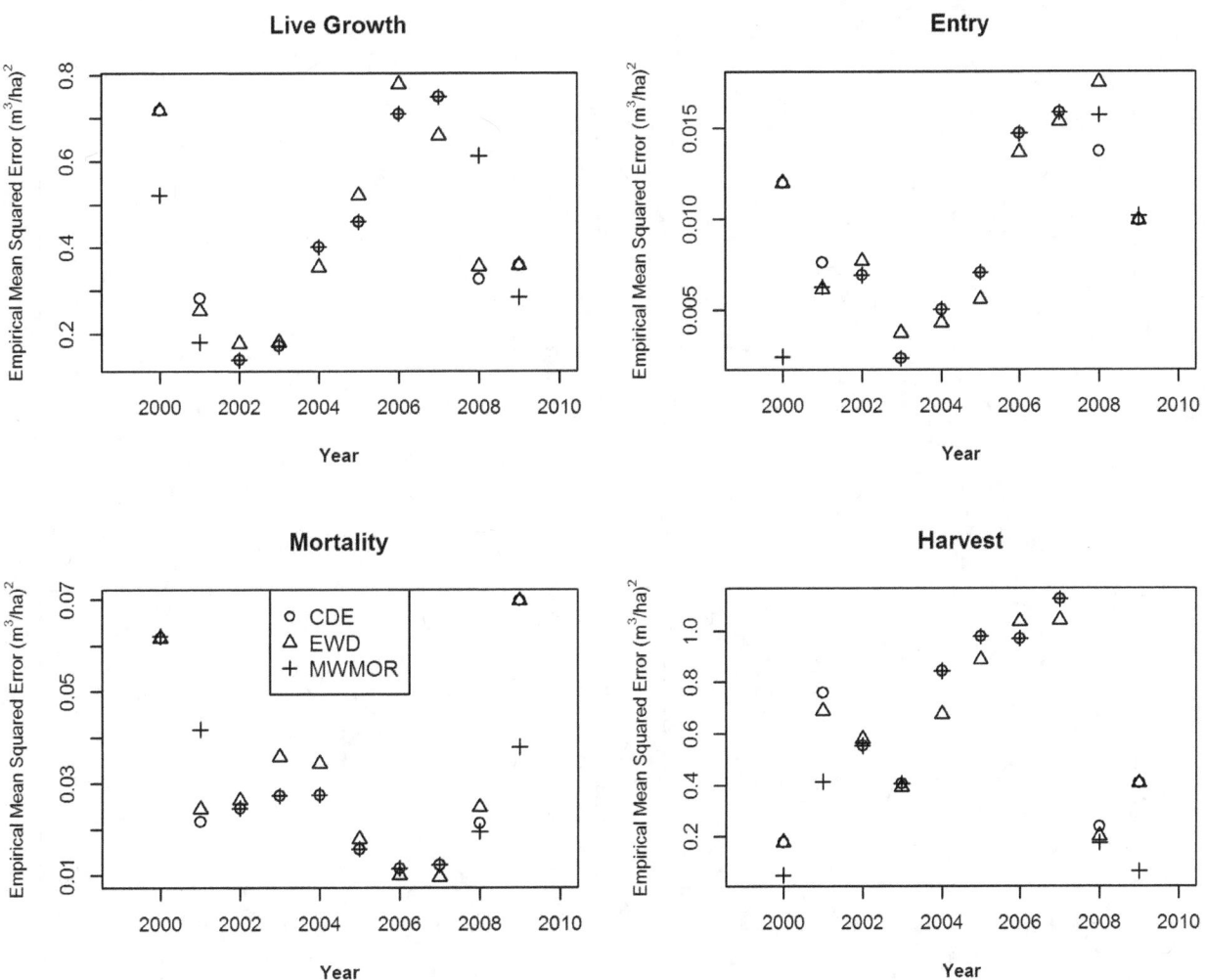

Figure 14E—The empirical mean squared error, over 1,000 iterations of 1,000 samples each from Population 1 under Sampling Error Structure 4, for the Centralized Difference Estimator (CDE), the Exponentially Weighted Difference (EWD) estimator, and the Moving-Windows Mean of Ratios (MWMOR) estimator, by growth component and estimation year.

Population 2 - Sample Error Structure 1

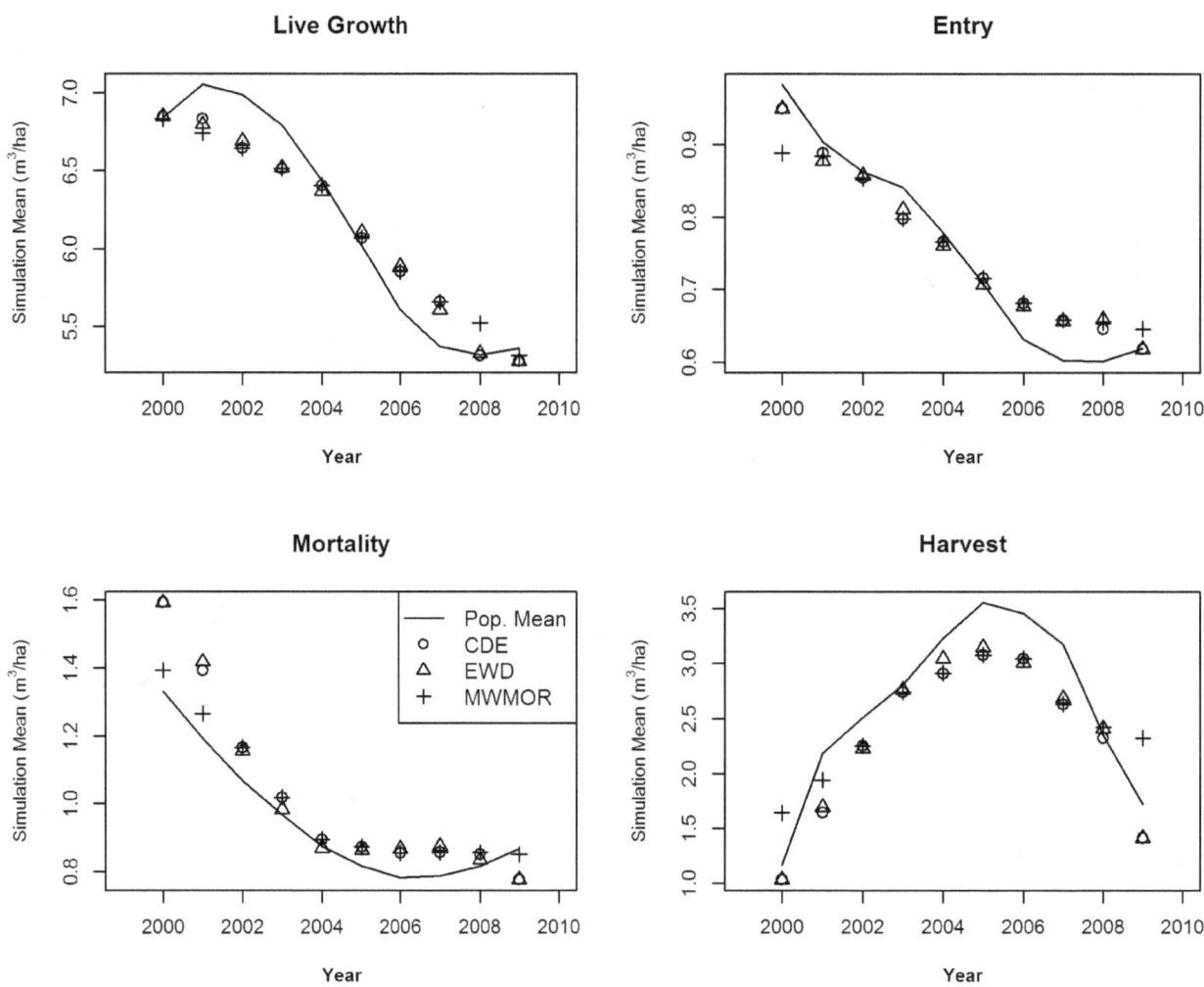

Figure 21M—The mean over 1,000 iterations of 1,000 samples each from Population 2 under Sampling Error Structure 1, for the Centralized Difference Estimator (CDE), the Exponentially Weighted Difference (EWD) estimator, and the Moving-Windows Mean of Ratios (MWMOR) estimator, by growth component and estimation year.

Population 2 - Sample Error Structure 1

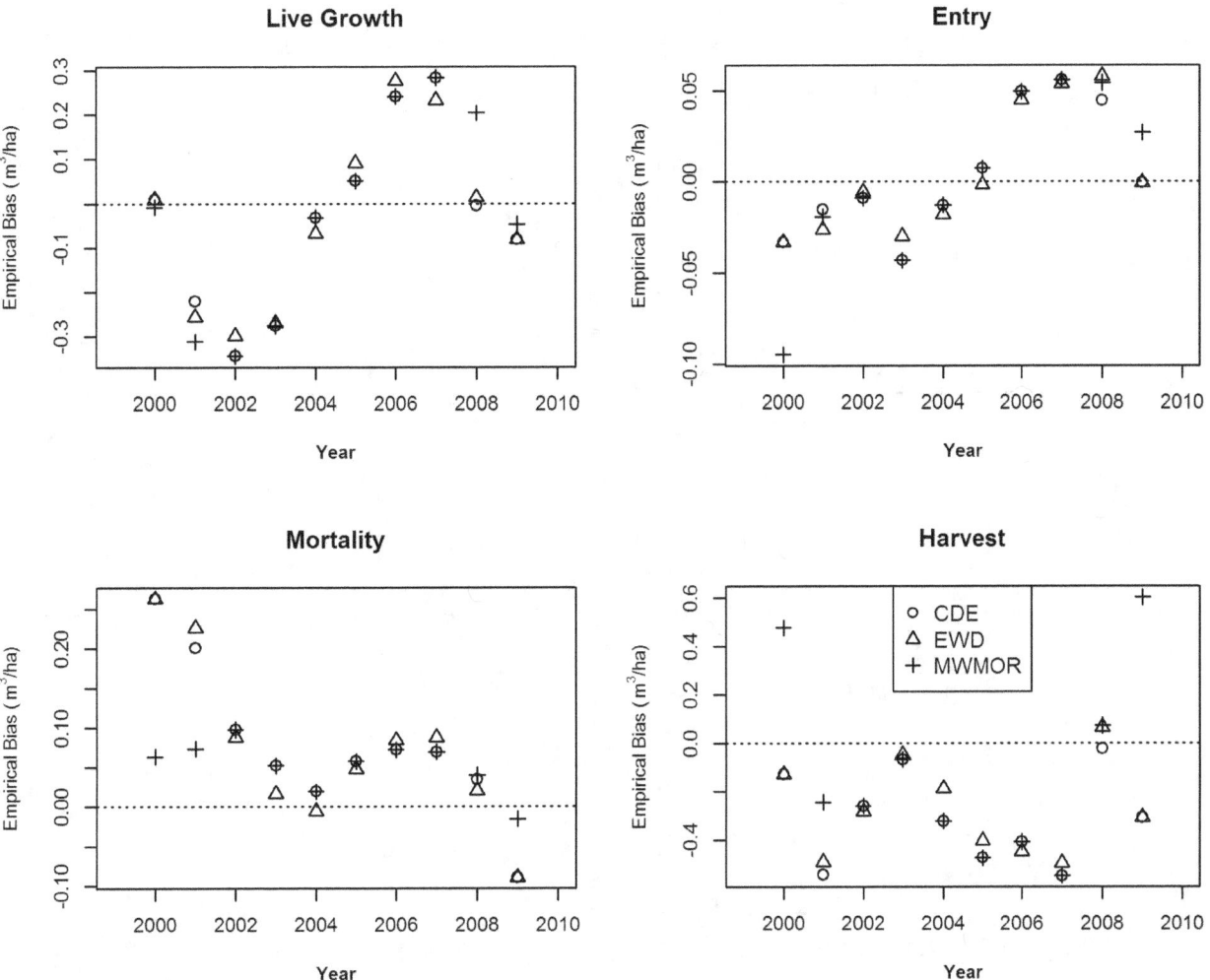

Figure 21B—The empirical bias, over 1,000 iterations of 1,000 samples each from Population 2 under Sampling Error Structure 1, for the Centralized Difference Estimator (CDE), the Exponentially Weighted Difference (EWD) estimator, and the Moving-Windows Mean of Ratios (MWMOR) estimator, by growth component and estimation year.

Population 2 - Sample Error Structure 1

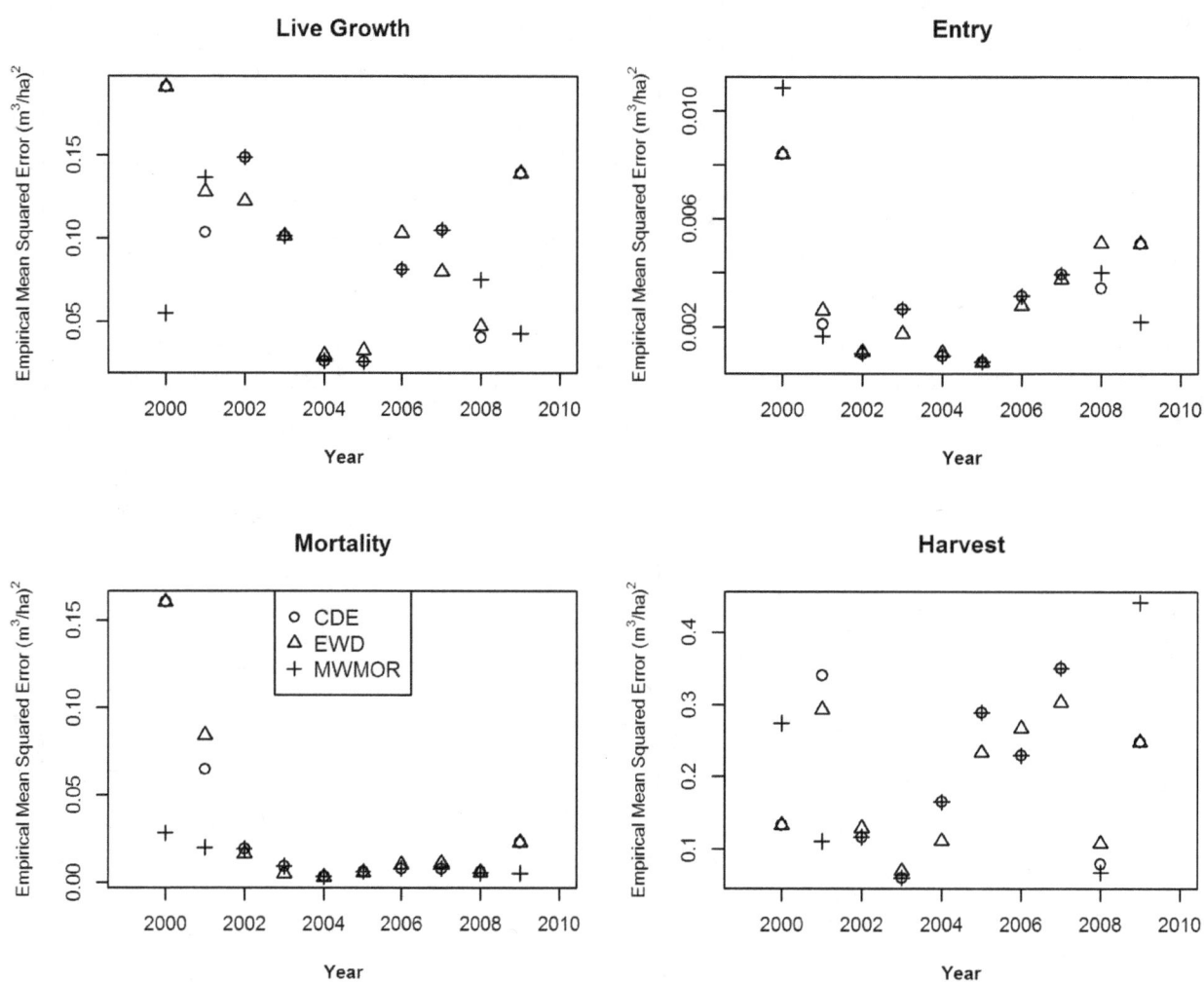

Figure 21E—The empirical mean squared error, over 1,000 iterations of 1,000 samples each from Population 2 under Sampling Error Structure 1, for the Centralized Difference Estimator (CDE), the Exponentially Weighted Difference (EWD) estimator, and the Moving-Windows Mean of Ratios (MWMOR) estimator, by growth component and estimation year.

Population 2 - Sample Error Structure 2

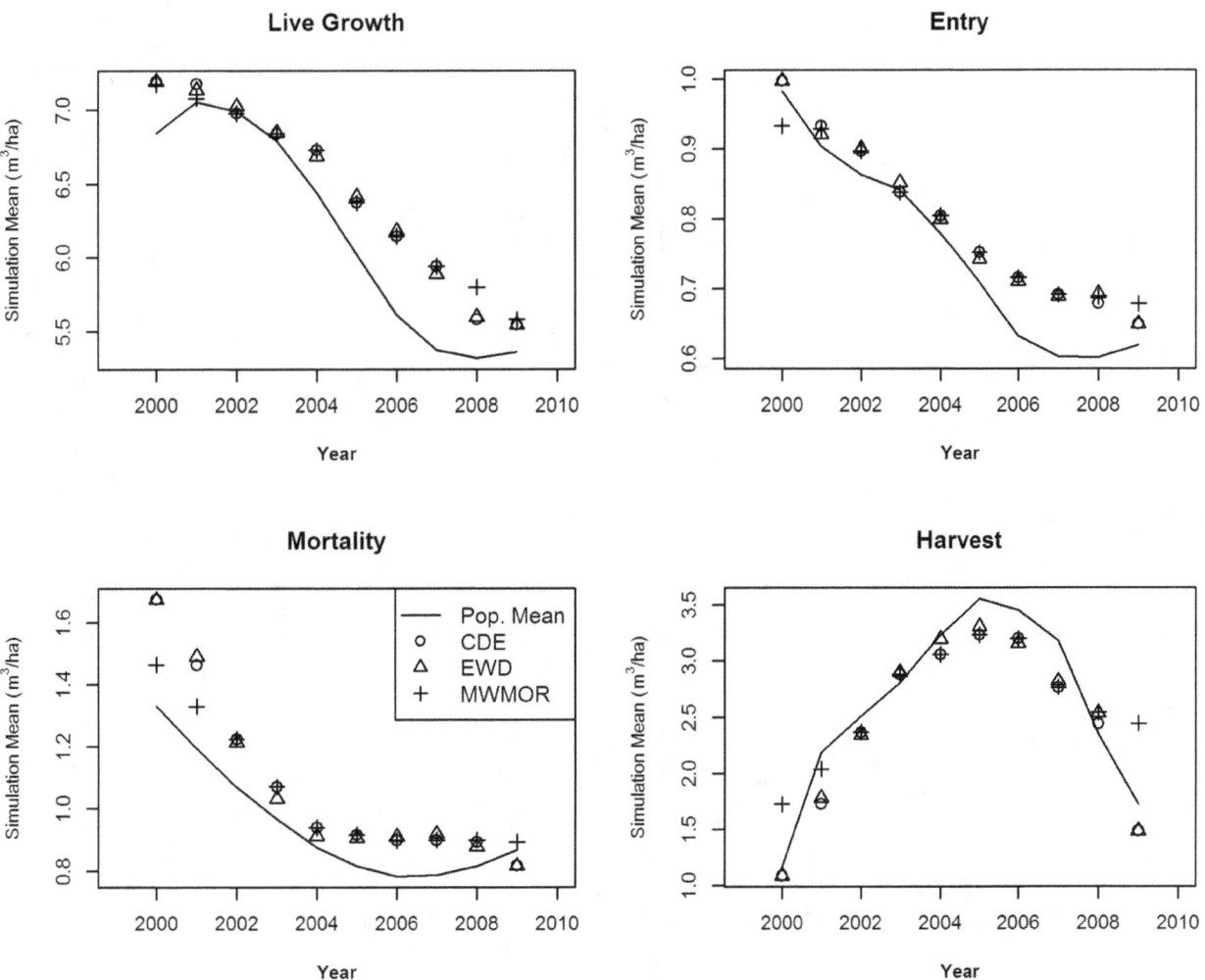

Figure 22M—The mean over 1,000 iterations of 1,000 samples each from Population 2 under Sampling Error Structure 2, for the Centralized Difference Estimator (CDE), the Exponentially Weighted Difference (EWD) estimator, and the Moving-Windows Mean of Ratios (MWMOR) estimator, by growth component and estimation year.

Population 2 - Sample Error Structure 2

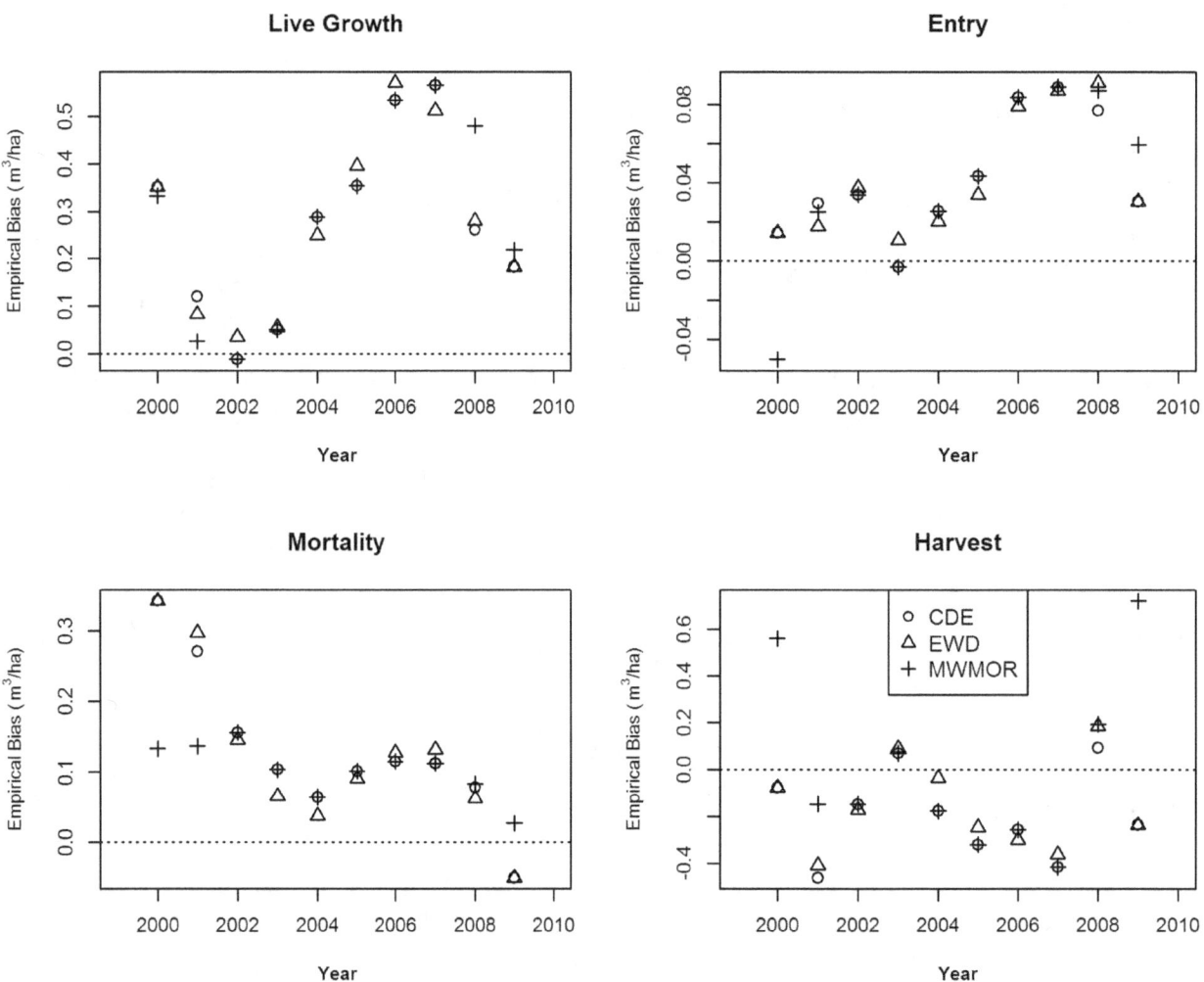

Figure 22B—The empirical bias, over 1,000 iterations of 1,000 samples each from Population 2 under Sampling Error Structure 2, for the Centralized Difference Estimator (CDE), the Exponentially Weighted Difference (EWD) estimator, and the Moving-Windows Mean of Ratios (MWMOR) estimator, by growth component and estimation year.

Population 2 - Sample Error Structure 2

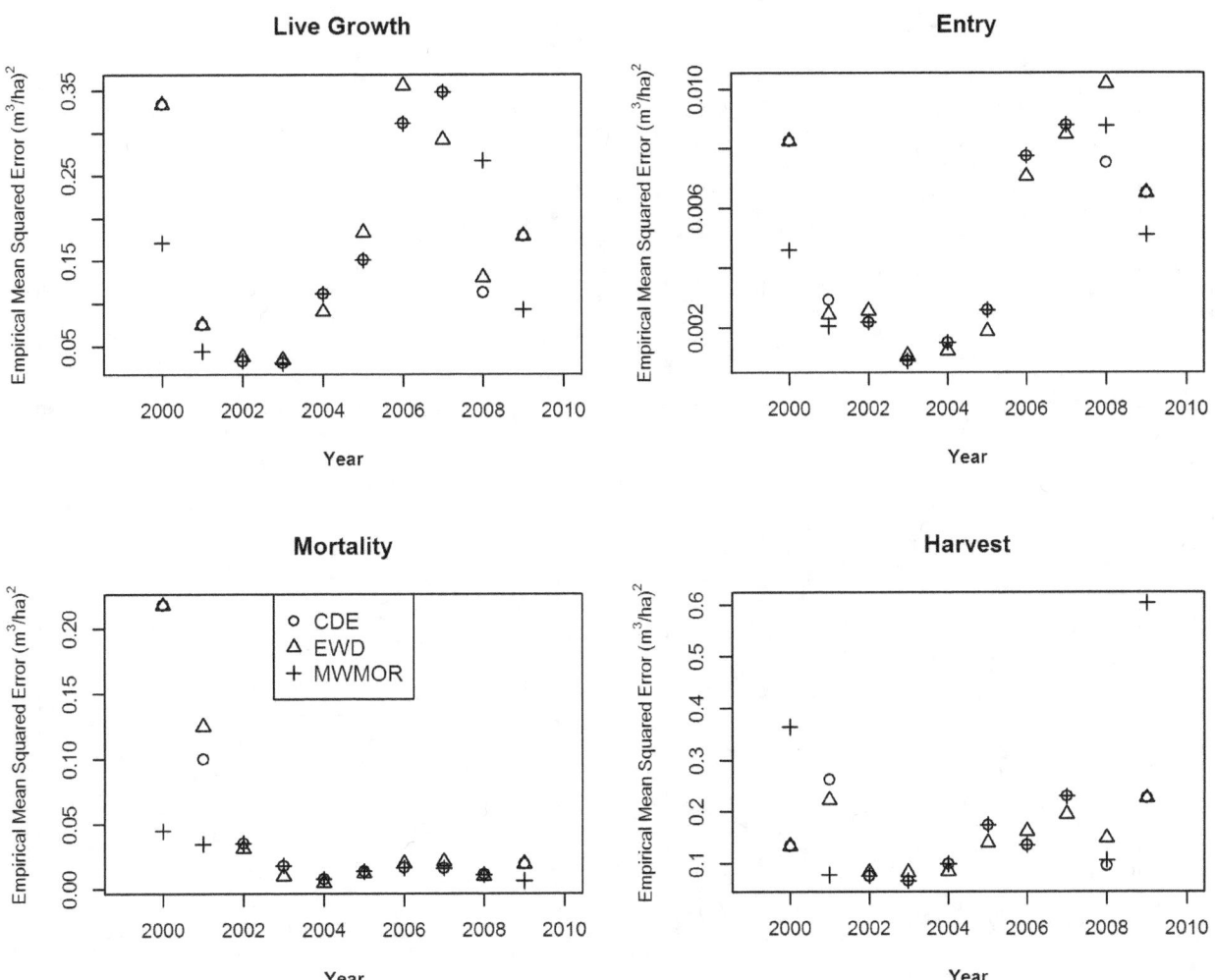

Figure 22E—The empirical mean squared error, over 1,000 iterations of 1,000 samples each from Population 2 under Sampling Error Structure 2, for the Centralized Difference Estimator (CDE), the Exponentially Weighted Difference (EWD) estimator, and the Moving-Windows Mean of Ratios (MWMOR) estimator, by growth component and estimation year.

Population 2 - Sample Error Structure 3

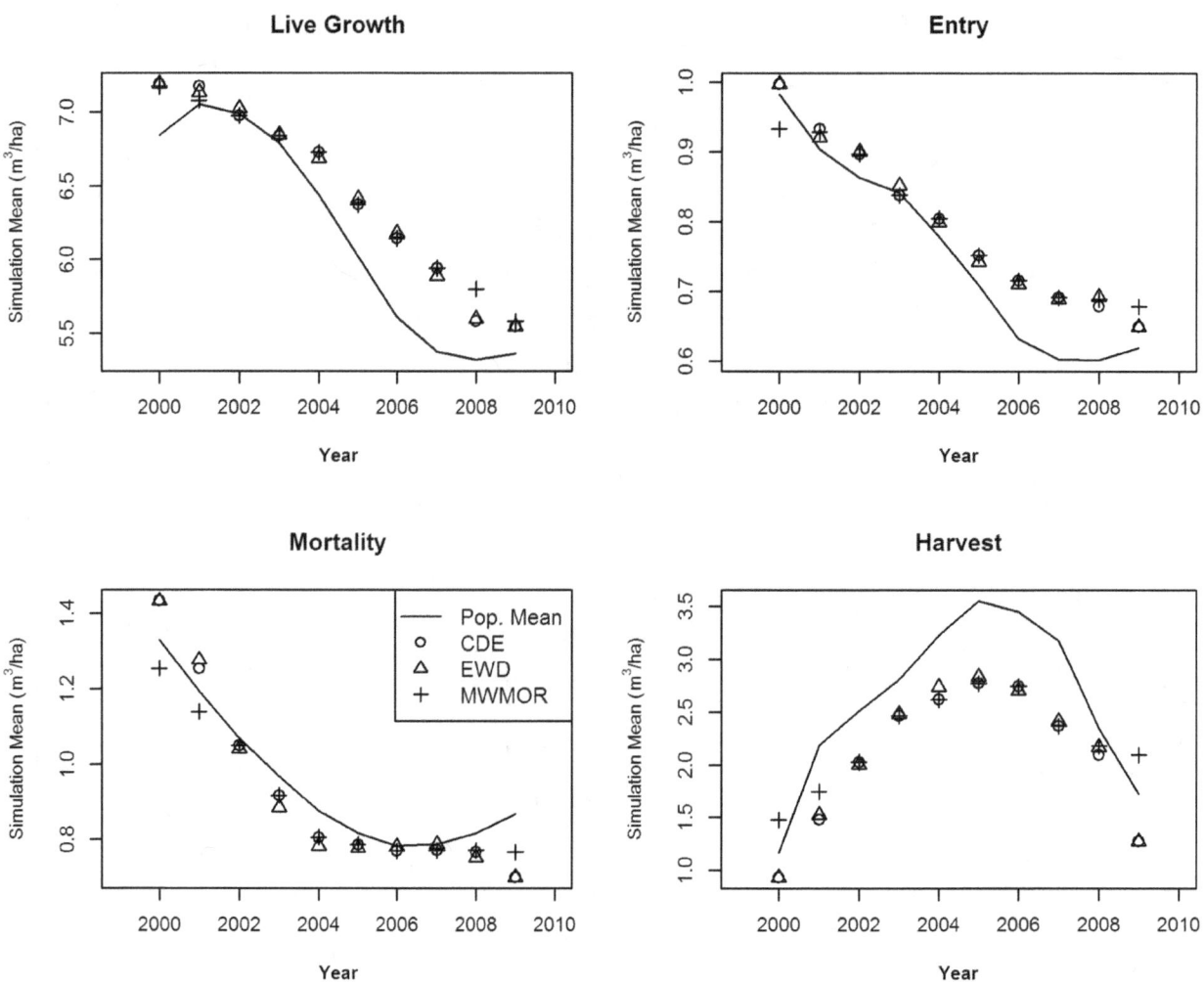

Figure 23M—The mean over 1,000 iterations of 1,000 samples each from Population 2 under Sampling Error Structure 3, for the Centralized Difference Estimator (CDE), the Exponentially Weighted Difference (EWD) estimator, and the Moving-Windows Mean of Ratios (MWMOR) estimator, by growth component and estimation year.

Population 2 - Sample Error Structure 3

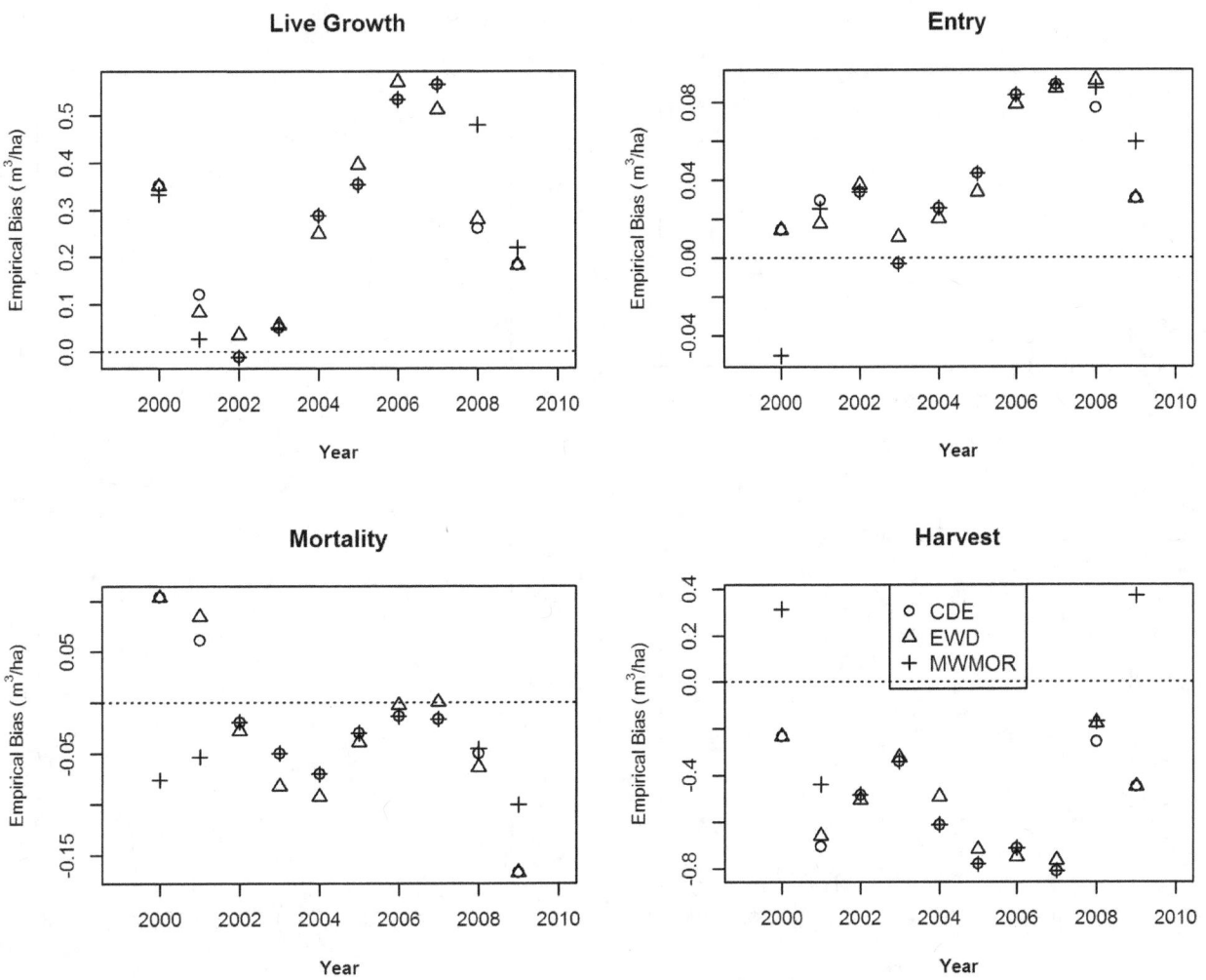

Figure 23B—The empirical bias, over 1,000 iterations of 1,000 samples each from Population 2 under Sampling Error Structure 3, for the Centralized Difference Estimator (CDE), the Exponentially Weighted Difference (EWD) estimator, and the Moving-Windows Mean of Ratios (MWMOR) estimator, by growth component and estimation year.

Population 2 - Sample Error Structure 3

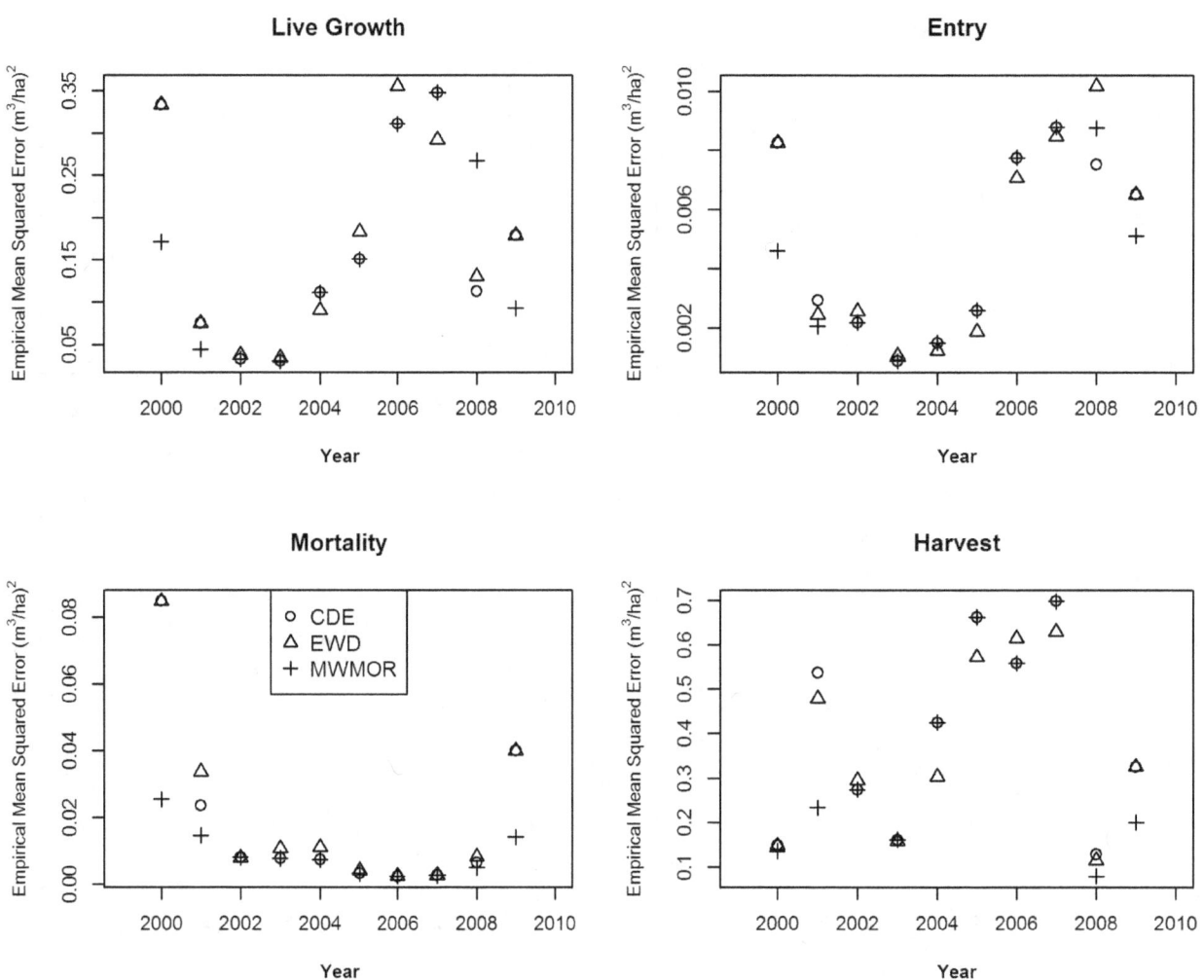

Figure 23E—The empirical mean squared error, over 1,000 iterations of 1,000 samples each from Population 2 under Sampling Error Structure 3, for the Centralized Difference Estimator (CDE), the Exponentially Weighted Difference (EWD) estimator, and the Moving-Windows Mean of Ratios (MWMOR) estimator, by growth component and estimation year.

Population 2 - Sample Error Structure 4

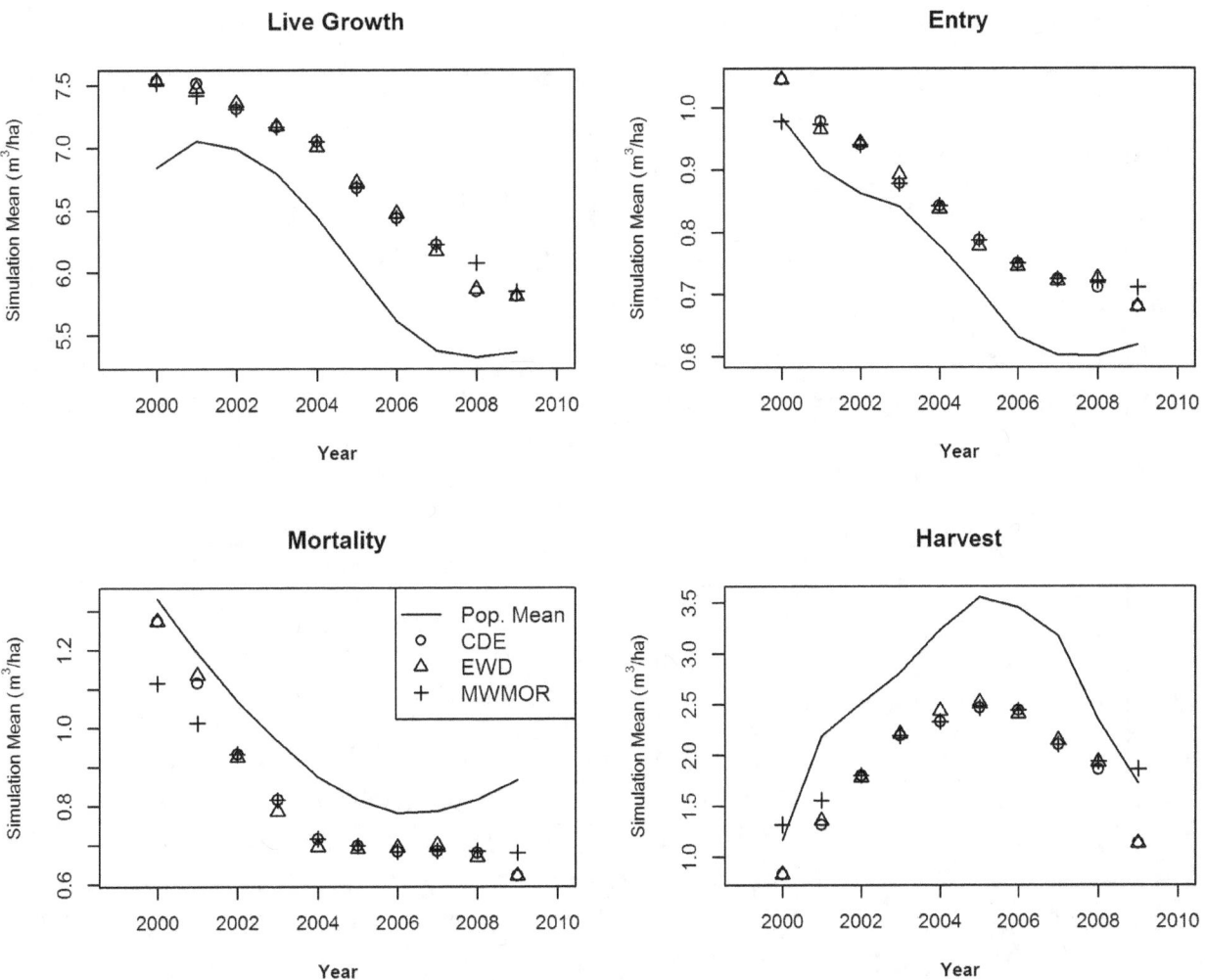

Figure 24M—The mean over 1,000 iterations of 1,000 samples each from Population 2 under Sampling Error Structure 4, for the Centralized Difference Estimator (CDE), the Exponentially Weighted Difference (EWD) estimator, and the Moving-Windows Mean of Ratios (MWMOR) estimator, by growth component and estimation year.

Population 2 - Sample Error Structure 4

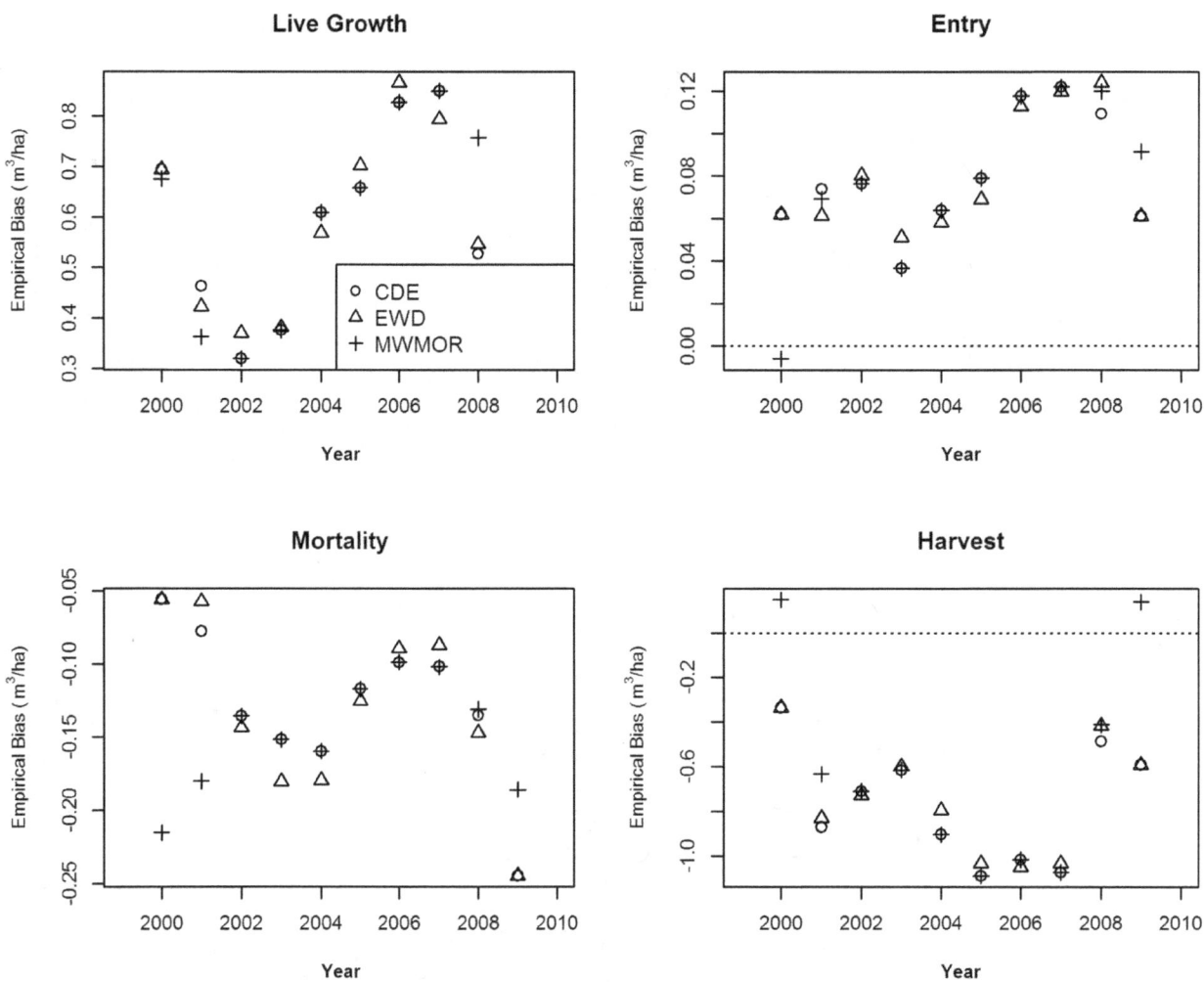

Figure 24B—The empirical bias, over 1,000 iterations of 1,000 samples each from Population 2 under Sampling Error Structure 4, for the Centralized Difference Estimator (CDE), the Exponentially Weighted Difference (EWD) estimator, and the Moving-Windows Mean of Ratios (MWMOR) estimator, by growth component and estimation year.

Population 2 - Sample Error Structure 4

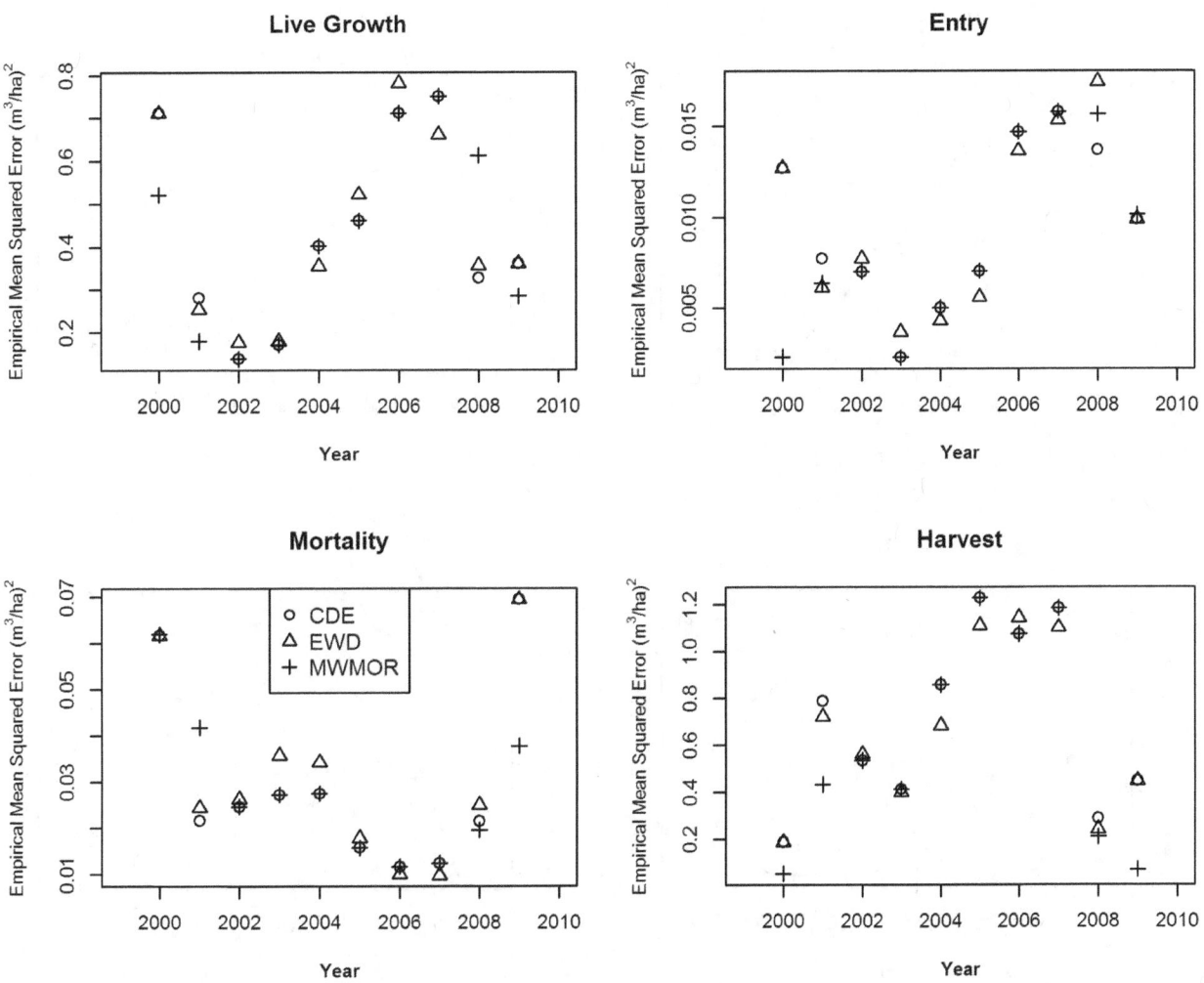

Figure 24E—The empirical mean squared error, over 1,000 iterations of 1,000 samples each from Population 2 under Sampling Error Structure 4, for the Centralized Difference Estimator (CDE), the Exponentially Weighted Difference (EWD) estimator, and the Moving-Windows Mean of Ratios (MWMOR) estimator, by growth component and estimation year.

Population 3 - Sample Error Structure 1

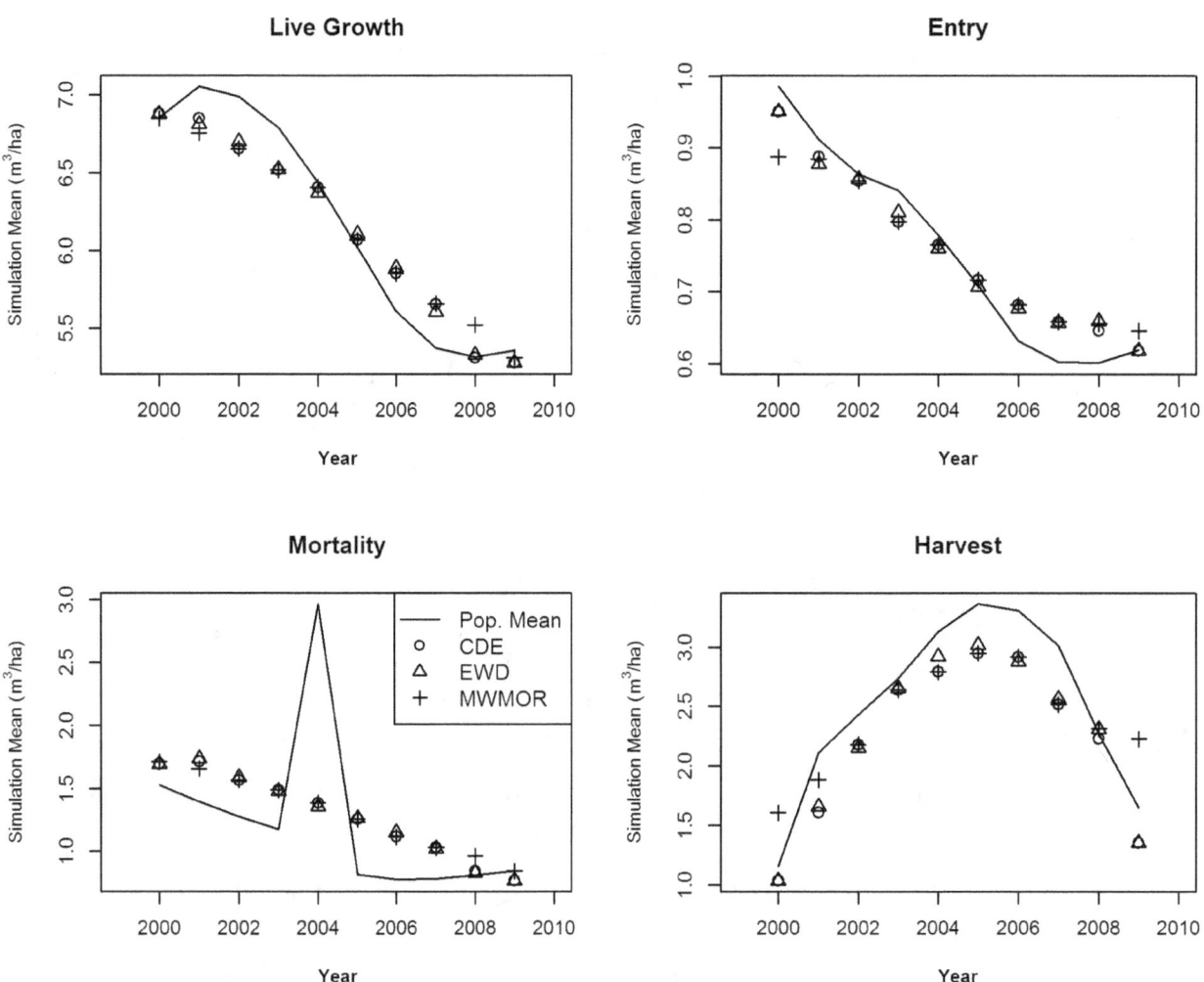

Figure 31M—The mean over 1,000 iterations of 1,000 samples each from Population 3 under Sampling Error Structure 1, for the Centralized Difference Estimator (CDE), the Exponentially Weighted Difference (EWD) estimator, and the Moving-Windows Mean of Ratios (MWMOR) estimator, by growth component and estimation year.

Population 3 - Sample Error Structure 1

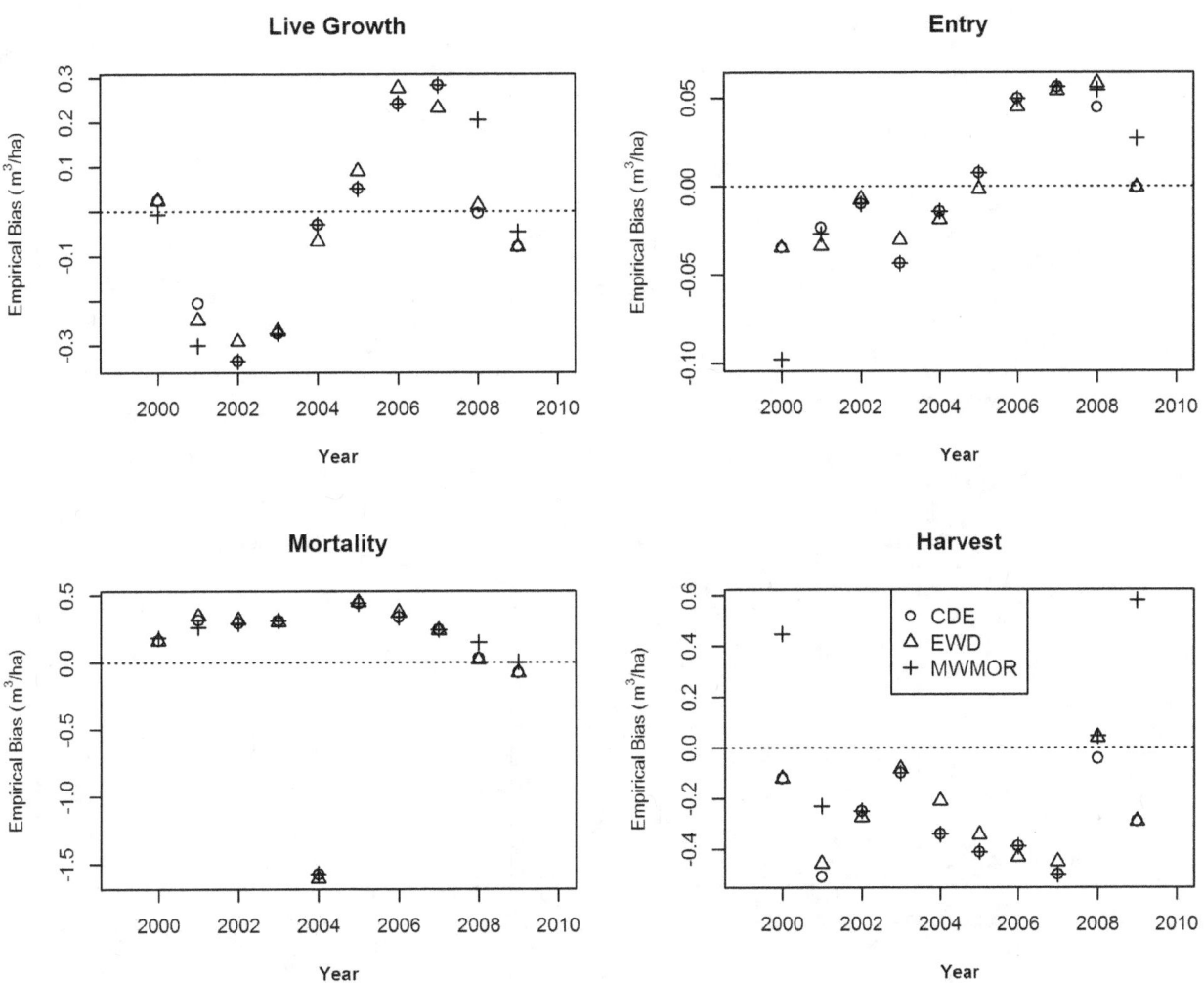

Figure 31B—The empirical bias, over 1,000 iterations of 1,000 samples each from Population 3 under Sampling Error Structure 1, for the Centralized Difference Estimator (CDE), the Exponentially Weighted Difference (EWD) estimator, and the Moving-Windows Mean of Ratios (MWMOR) estimator, by growth component and estimation year.

Population 3 - Sample Error Structure 1

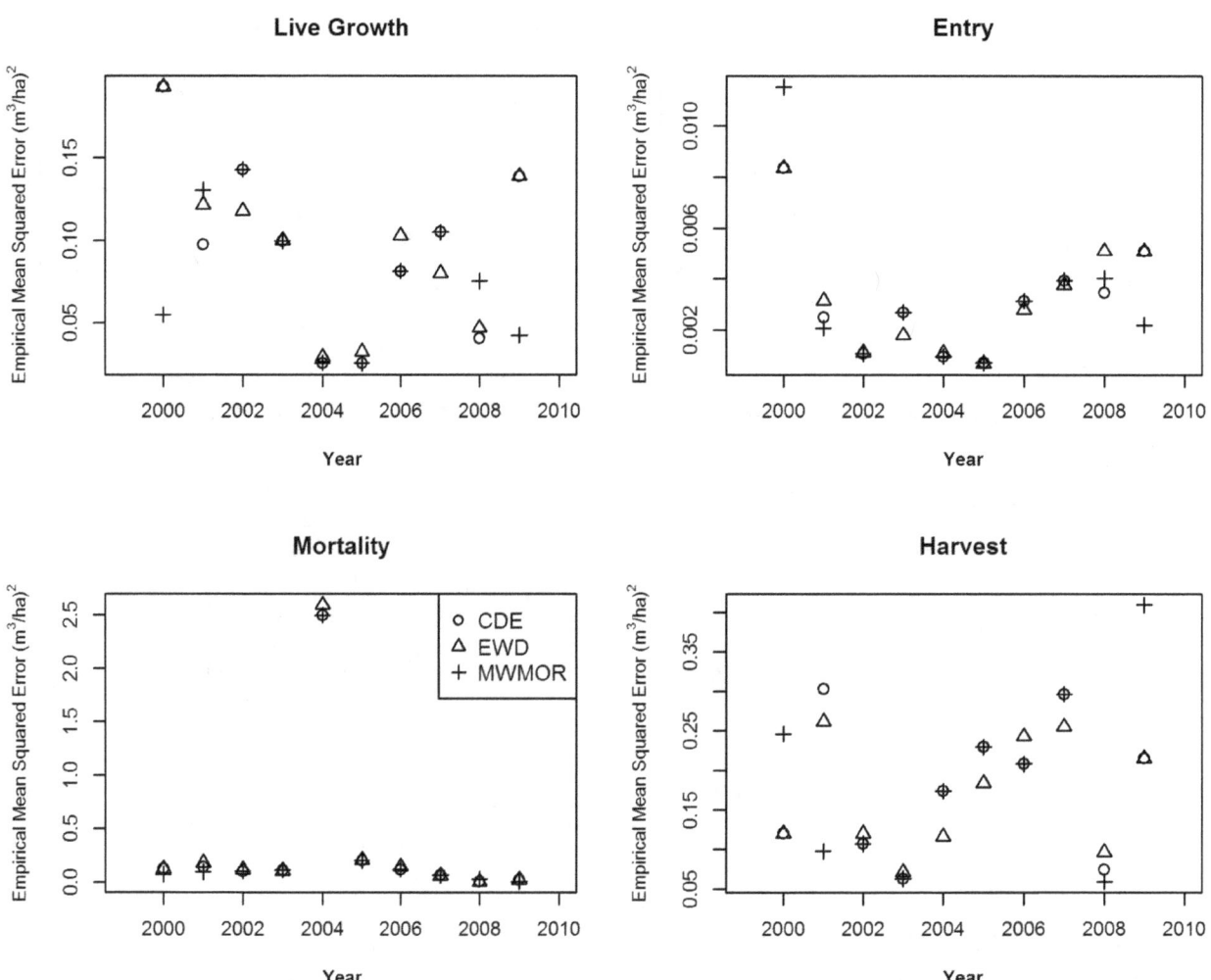

Figure 31E—The empirical mean squared error, over 1,000 iterations of 1,000 samples each from Population 3 under Sampling Error Structure 1, for the Centralized Difference Estimator (CDE), the Exponentially Weighted Difference (EWD) estimator, and the Moving-Windows Mean of Ratios (MWMOR) estimator, by growth component and estimation year.

Population 3 - Sample Error Structure 2

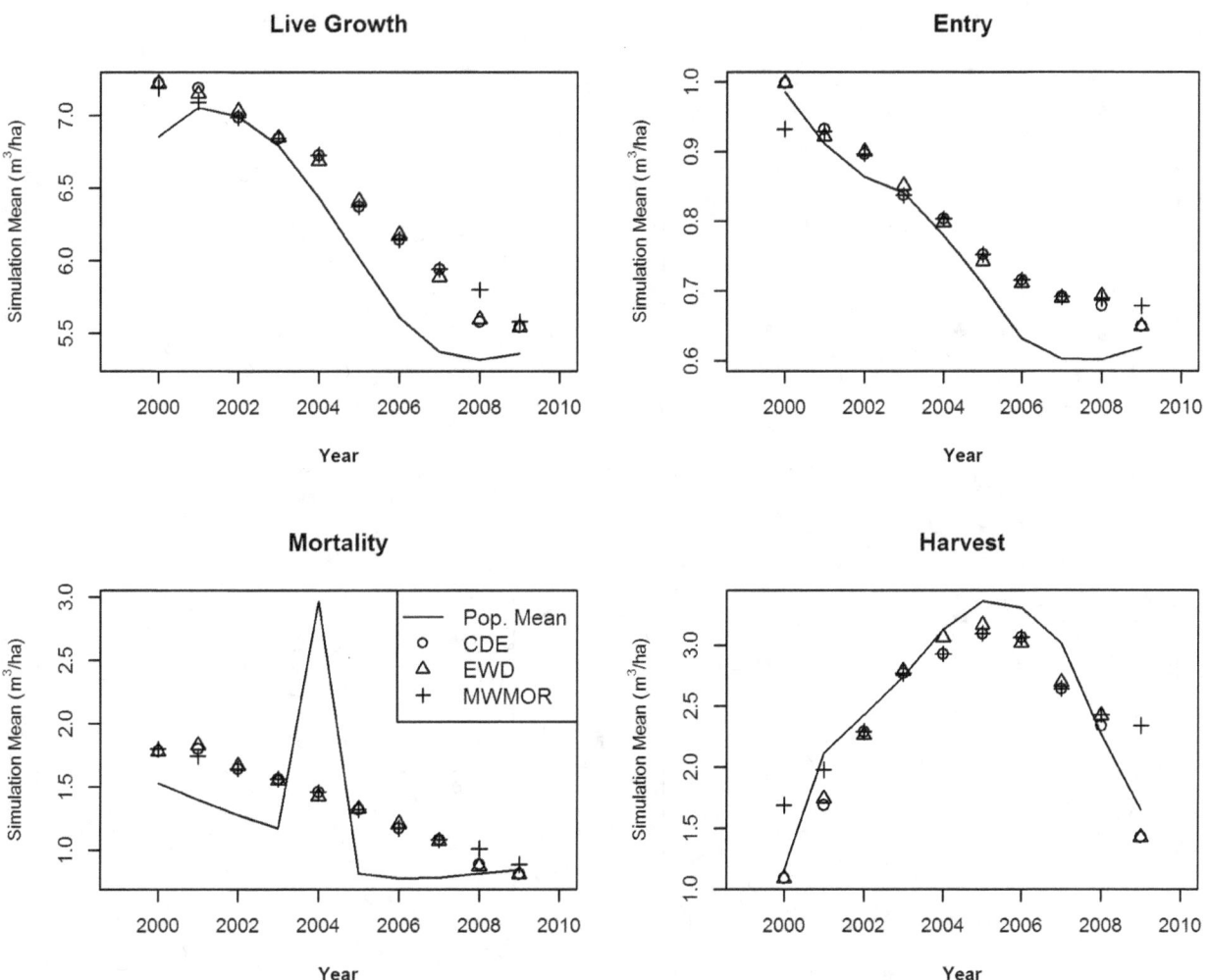

Figure 32M—The mean over 1,000 iterations of 1,000 samples each from Population 3 under Sampling Error Structure 2, for the Centralized Difference Estimator (CDE), the Exponentially Weighted Difference (EWD) estimator, and the Moving-Windows Mean of Ratios (MWMOR) estimator, by growth component and estimation year.

Population 3 - Sample Error Structure 2

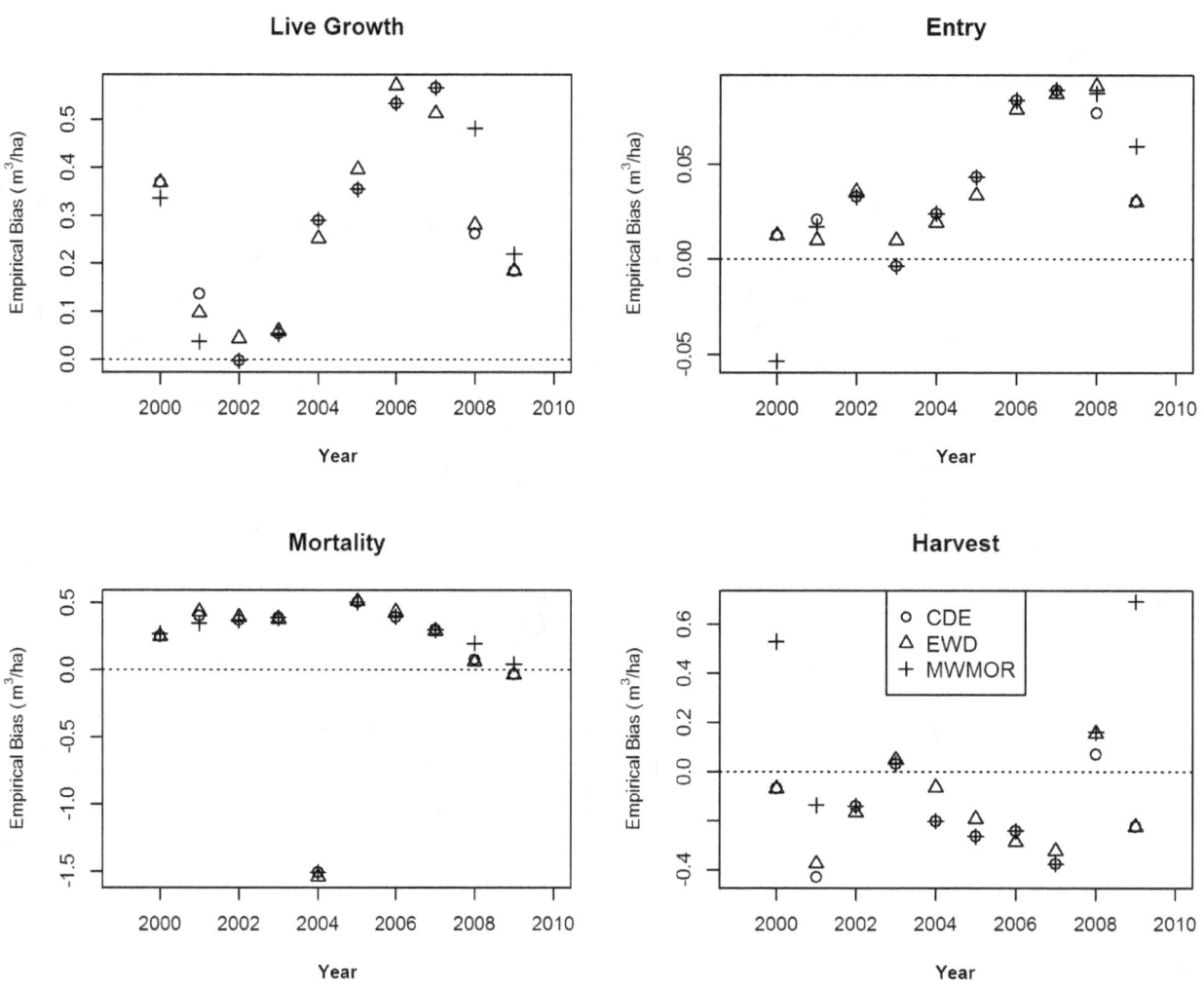

Figure 32B—The empirical bias, over 1,000 iterations of 1,000 samples each from Population 3 under Sampling Error Structure 2, for the Centralized Difference Estimator (CDE), the Exponentially Weighted Difference (EWD) estimator, and the Moving-Windows Mean of Ratios (MWMOR) estimator, by growth component and estimation year.

Population 3 - Sample Error Structure 2

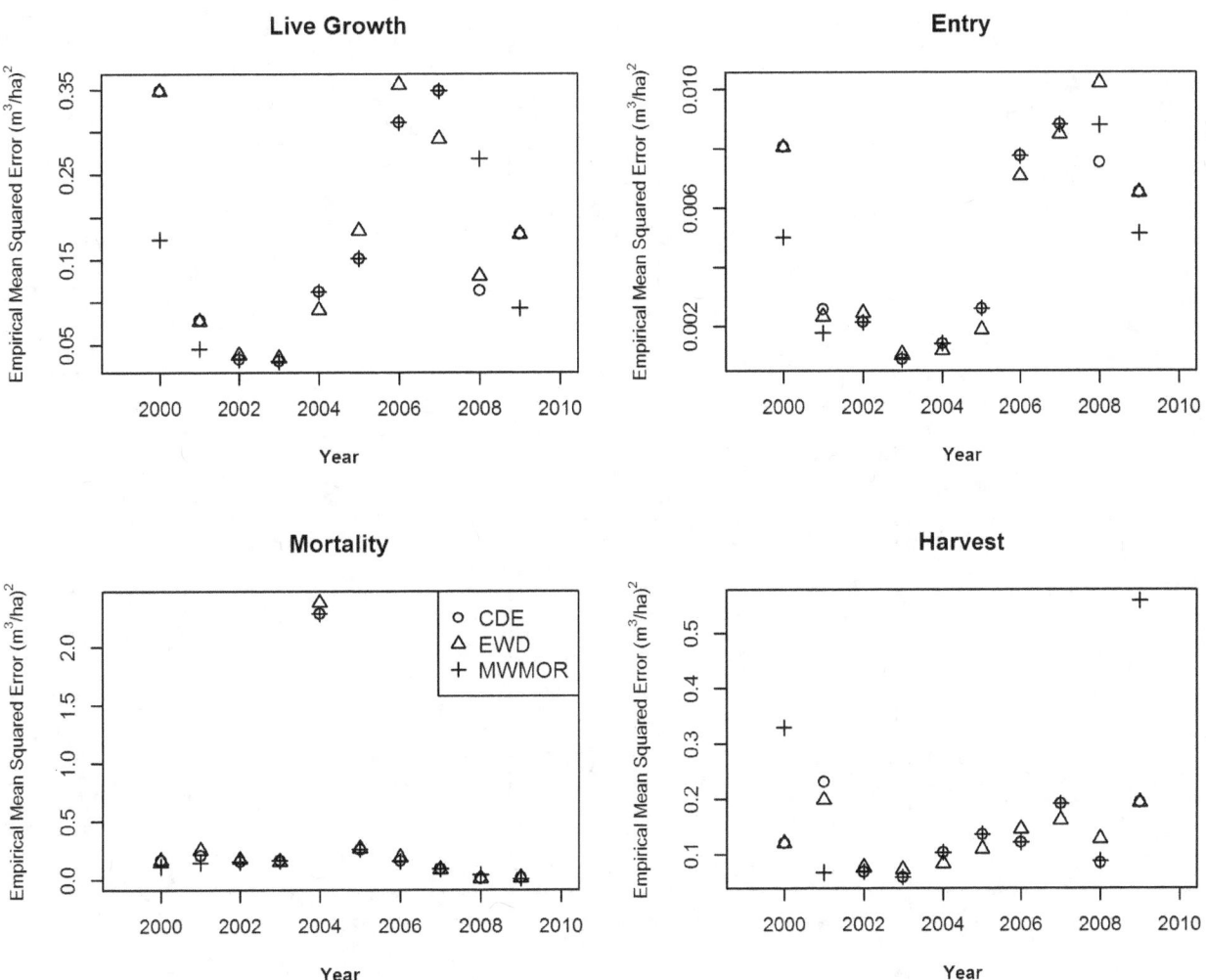

Figure 32E—The empirical mean squared error, over 1,000 iterations of 1,000 samples each from Population 3 under Sampling Error Structure 2, for the Centralized Difference Estimator (CDE), the Exponentially Weighted Difference (EWD) estimator, and the Moving-Windows Mean of Ratios (MWMOR) estimator, by growth component and estimation year.

Population 3 - Sample Error Structure 3

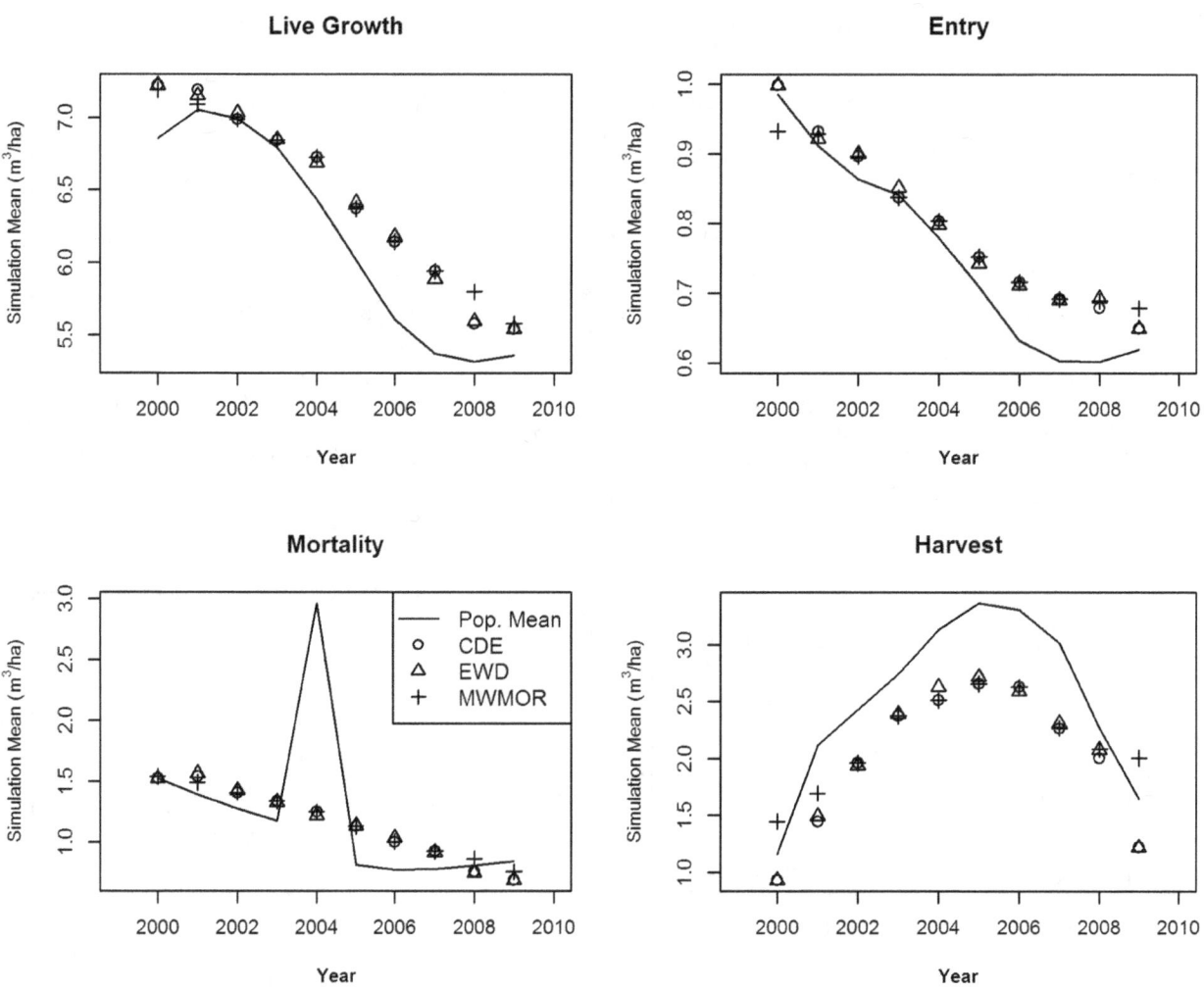

Figure 33M—The mean over 1,000 iterations of 1,000 samples each from Population 3 under Sampling Error Structure 3, for the Centralized Difference Estimator (CDE), the Exponentially Weighted Difference (EWD) estimator, and the Moving-Windows Mean of Ratios (MWMOR) estimator, by growth component and estimation year.

Population 3 - Sample Error Structure 3

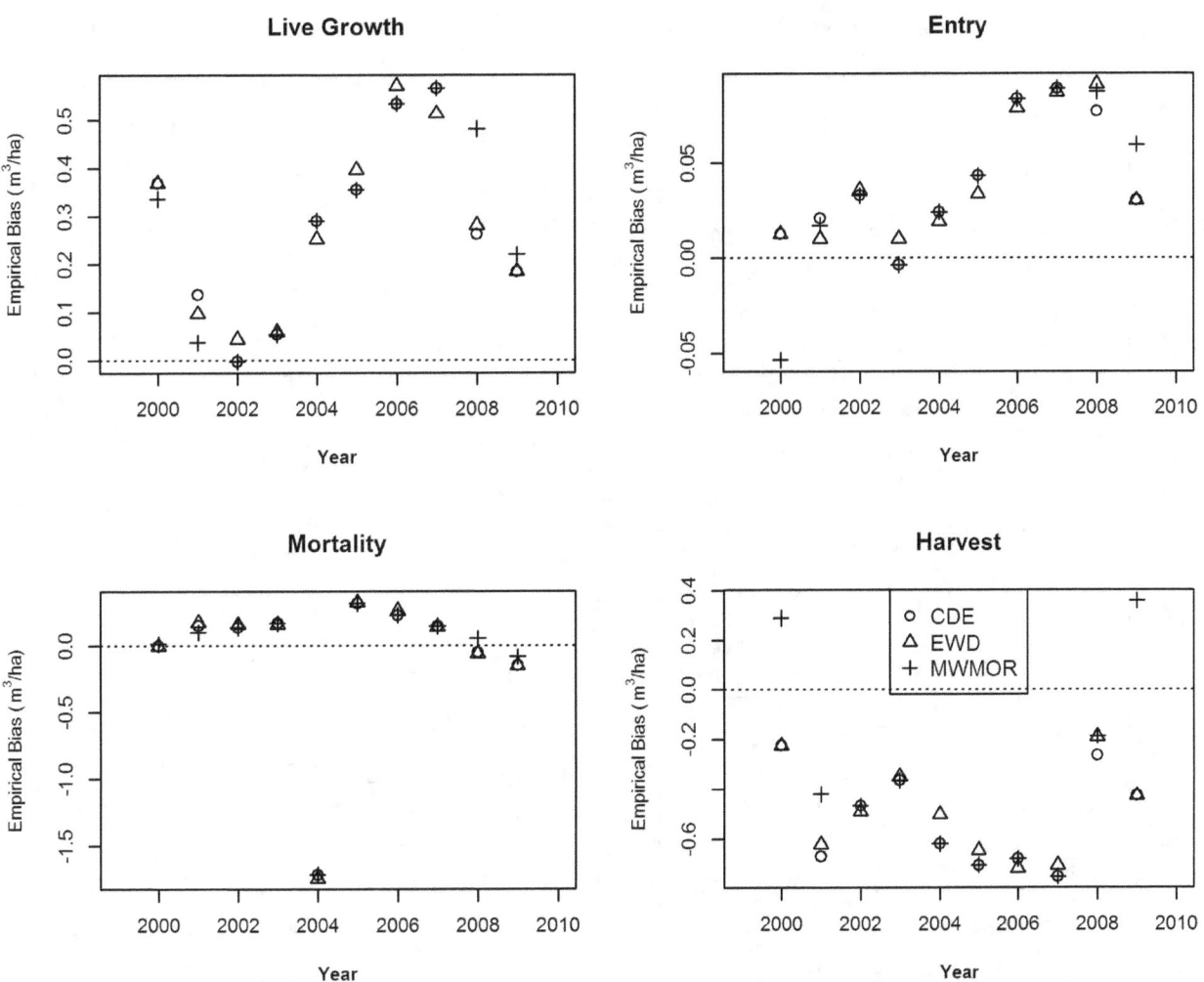

Figure 33B—The empirical bias, over 1,000 iterations of 1,000 samples each from Population 3 under Sampling Error Structure 3, for the Centralized Difference Estimator (CDE), the Exponentially Weighted Difference (EWD) estimator, and the Moving-Windows Mean of Ratios (MWMOR) estimator, by growth component and estimation year.

Population 3 - Sample Error Structure 3

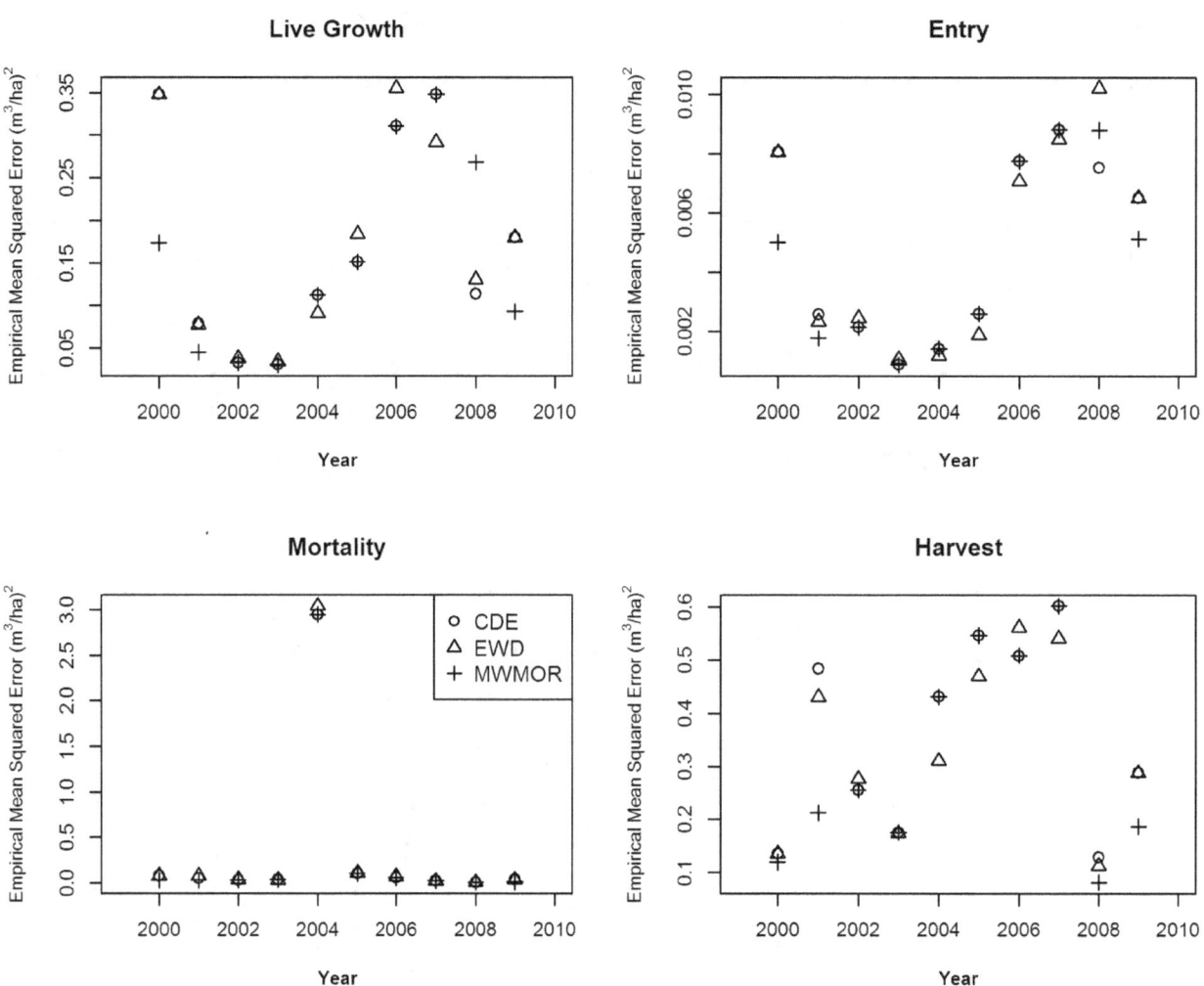

Figure 33E—The empirical mean squared error, over 1,000 iterations of 1,000 samples each from Population 3 under Sampling Error Structure 3, for the Centralized Difference Estimator (CDE), the Exponentially Weighted Difference (EWD) estimator, and the Moving-Windows Mean of Ratios (MWMOR) estimator, by growth component and estimation year.

Population 3 - Sample Error Structure 4

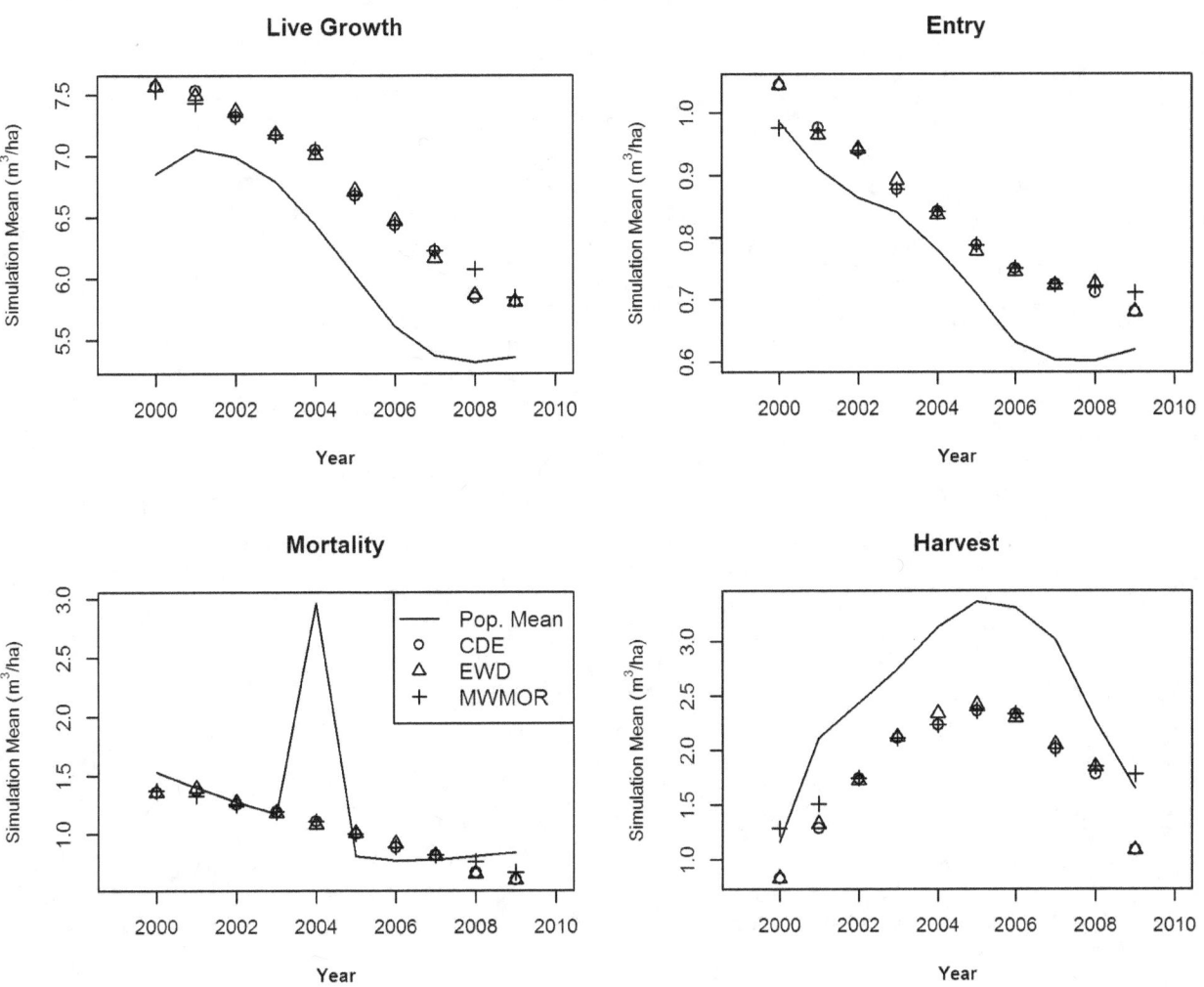

Figure 34M—The mean over 1,000 iterations of 1,000 samples each from Population 3 under Sampling Error Structure 4, for the Centralized Difference Estimator (CDE), the Exponentially Weighted Difference (EWD) estimator, and the Moving-Windows Mean of Ratios (MWMOR) estimator, by growth component and estimation year.

Population 3 - Sample Error Structure 4

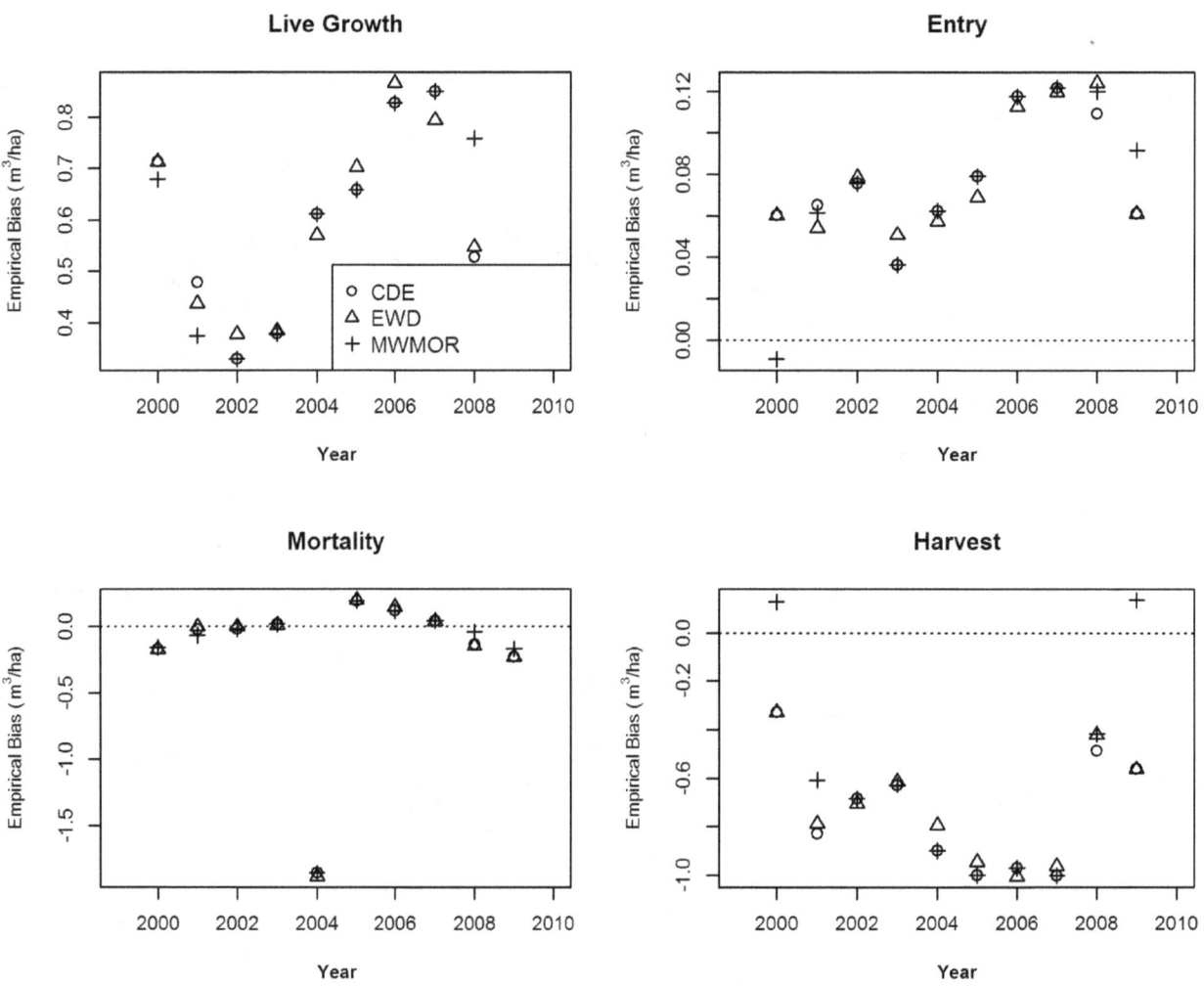

Figure 34B—The empirical bias, over 1,000 iterations of 1,000 samples each from Population 3 under Sampling Error Structure 4, for the Centralized Difference Estimator (CDE), the Exponentially Weighted Difference (EWD) estimator, and the Moving-Windows Mean of Ratios (MWMOR) estimator, by growth component and estimation year.

Population 3 - Sample Error Structure 4

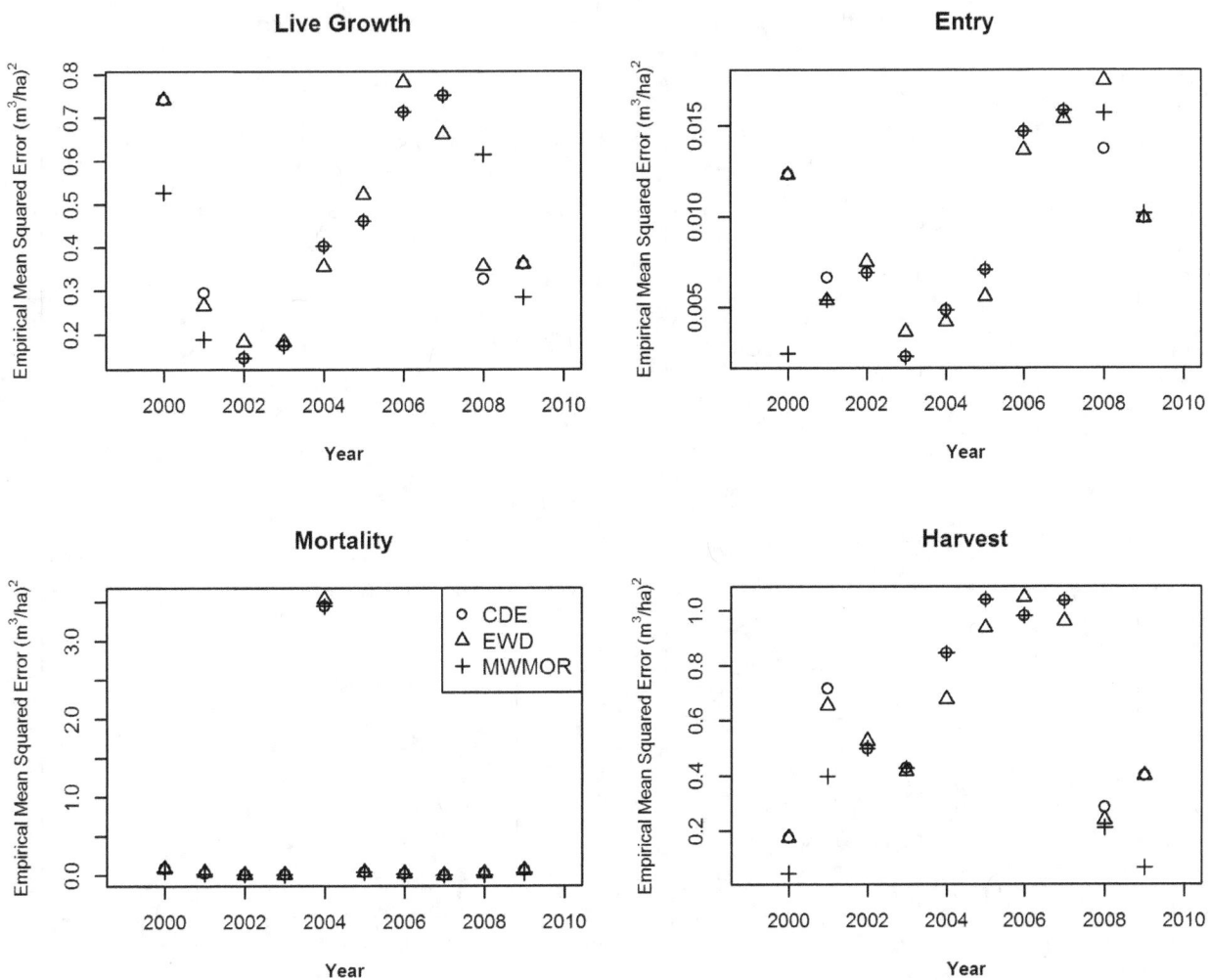

Figure 34E—The empirical mean squared error, over 1,000 iterations of 1,000 samples each from Population 3 under Sampling Error Structure 4, for the Centralized Difference Estimator (CDE), the Exponentially Weighted Difference (EWD) estimator, and the Moving-Windows Mean of Ratios (MWMOR) estimator, by growth component and estimation year.

Population 4 - Sample Error Structure 1

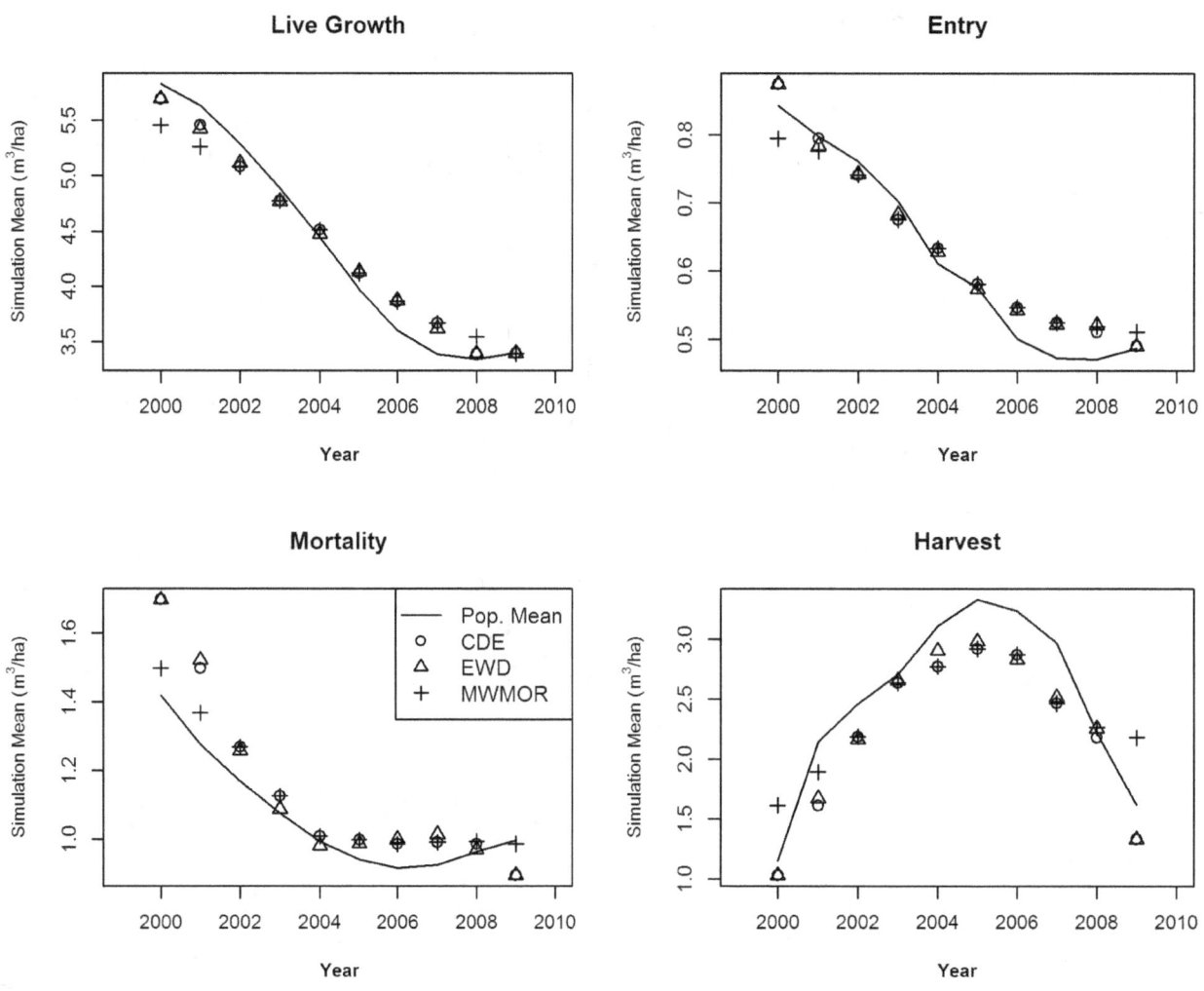

Figure 41M—The mean over 1,000 iterations of 1,000 samples each from Population 4 under Sampling Error Structure 1, for the Centralized Difference Estimator (CDE), the Exponentially Weighted Difference (EWD) estimator, and the Moving-Windows Mean of Ratios (MWMOR) estimator, by growth component and estimation year.

Population 4 - Sample Error Structure 1

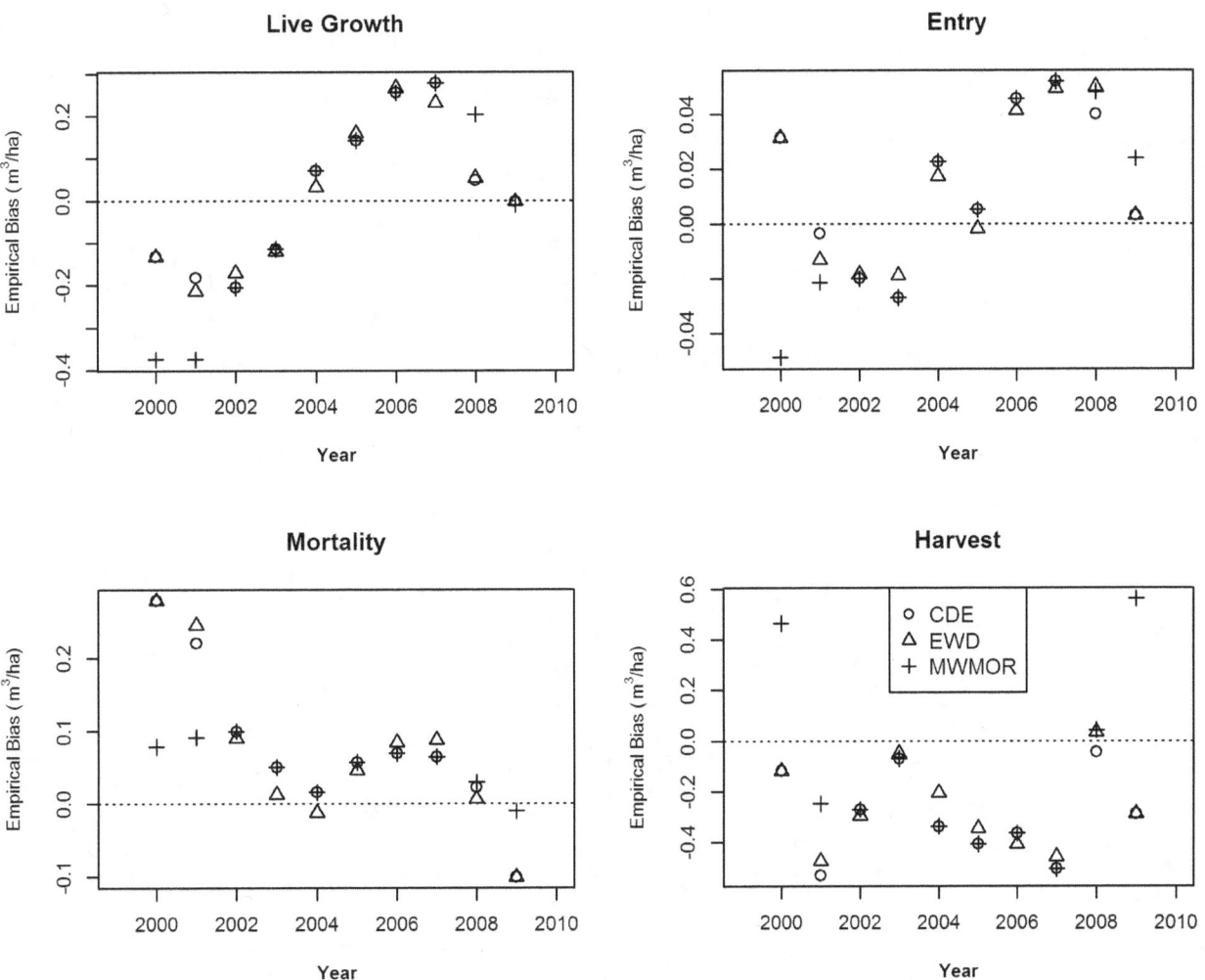

Figure 41B—The empirical bias, over 1,000 iterations of 1,000 samples each from Population 4 under Sampling Error Structure 1, for the Centralized Difference Estimator (CDE), the Exponentially Weighted Difference (EWD) estimator, and the Moving-Windows Mean of Ratios (MWMOR) estimator, by growth component and estimation year.

Population 4 - Sample Error Structure 1

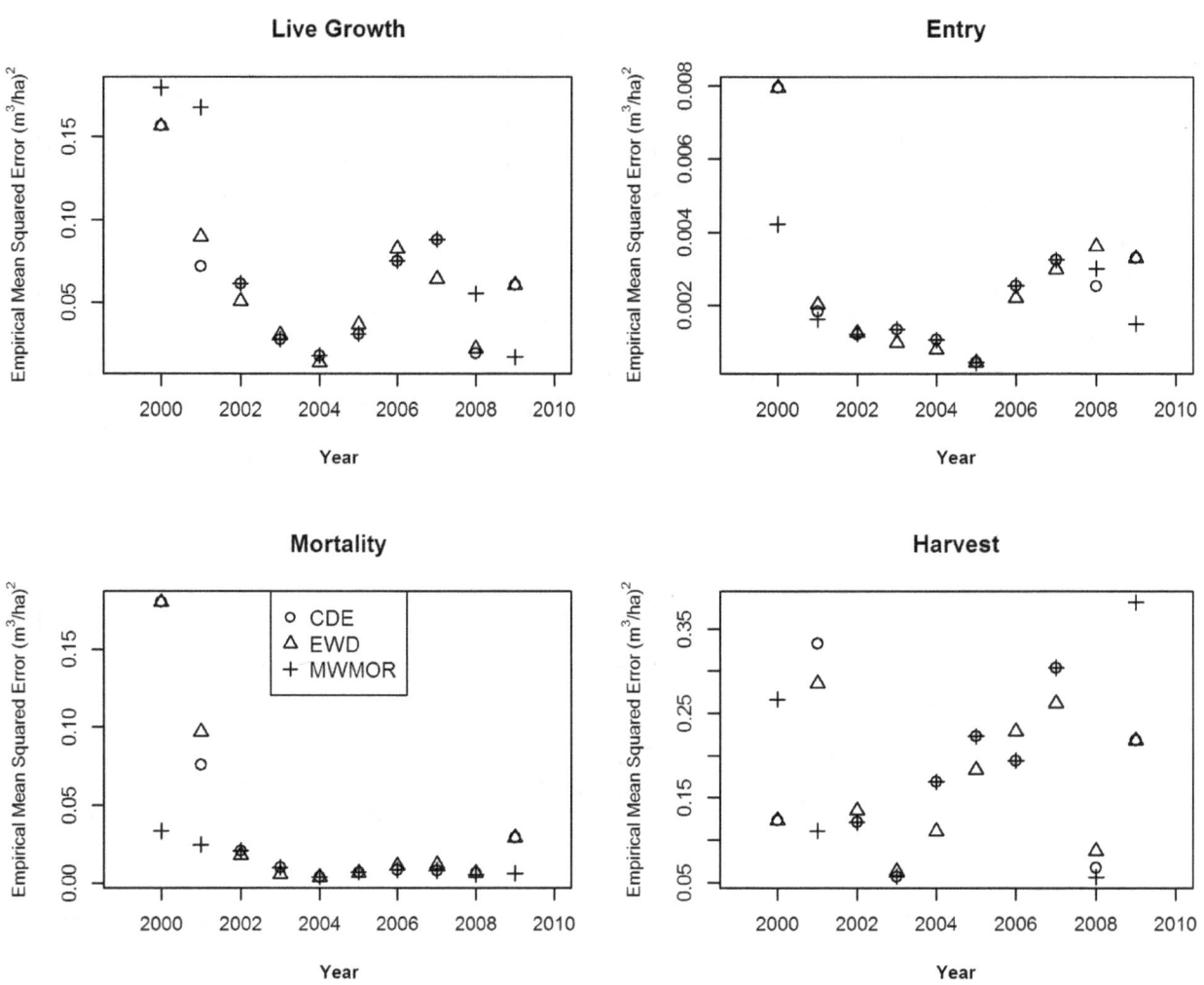

Figure 41E—The empirical mean squared error, over 1,000 iterations of 1,000 samples each from Population 4 under Sampling Error Structure 1, for the Centralized Difference Estimator (CDE), the Exponentially Weighted Difference (EWD) estimator, and the Moving-Windows Mean of Ratios (MWMOR) estimator, by growth component and estimation year.

Population 4 - Sample Error Structure 2

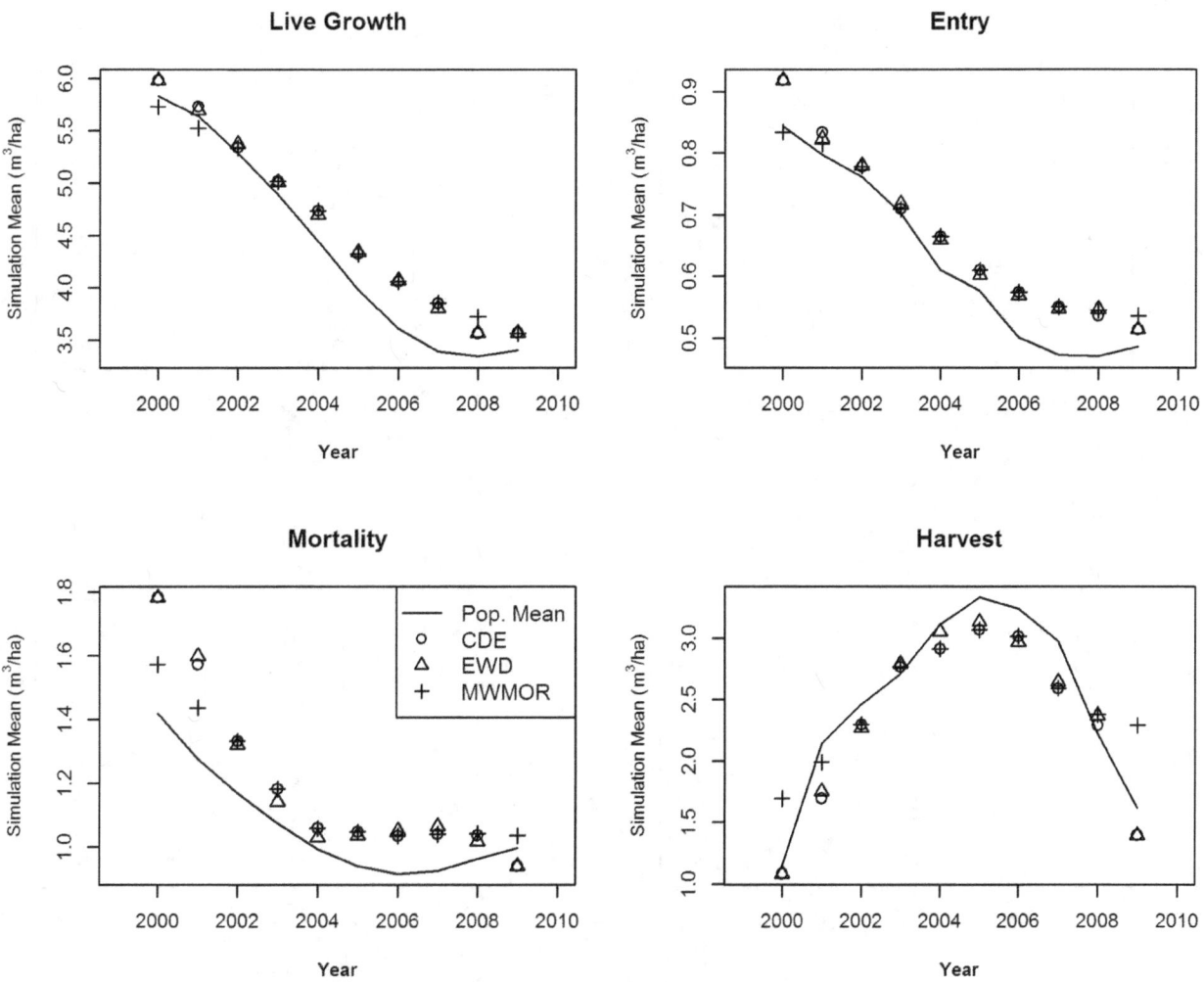

Figure 42M—The mean over 1,000 iterations of 1,000 samples each from Population 4 under Sampling Error Structure 2, for the Centralized Difference Estimator (CDE), the Exponentially Weighted Difference (EWD) estimator, and the Moving-Windows Mean of Ratios (MWMOR) estimator, by growth component and estimation year.

Population 4 - Sample Error Structure 2

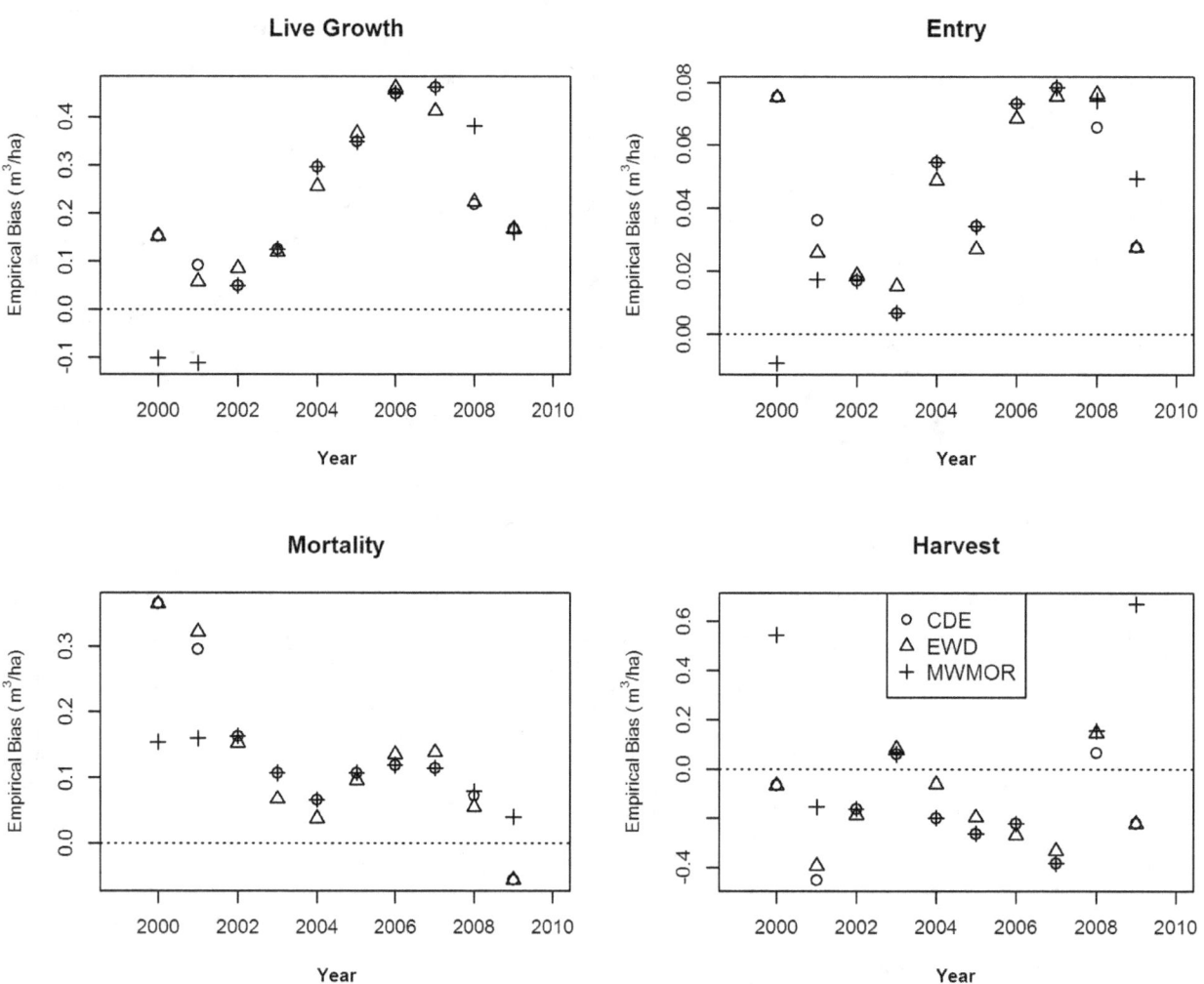

Figure 42B—The empirical bias, over 1,000 iterations of 1,000 samples each from Population 4 under Sampling Error Structure 2, for the Centralized Difference Estimator (CDE), the Exponentially Weighted Difference (EWD) estimator, and the Moving-Windows Mean of Ratios (MWMOR) estimator, by growth component and estimation year.

Population 4 - Sample Error Structure 2

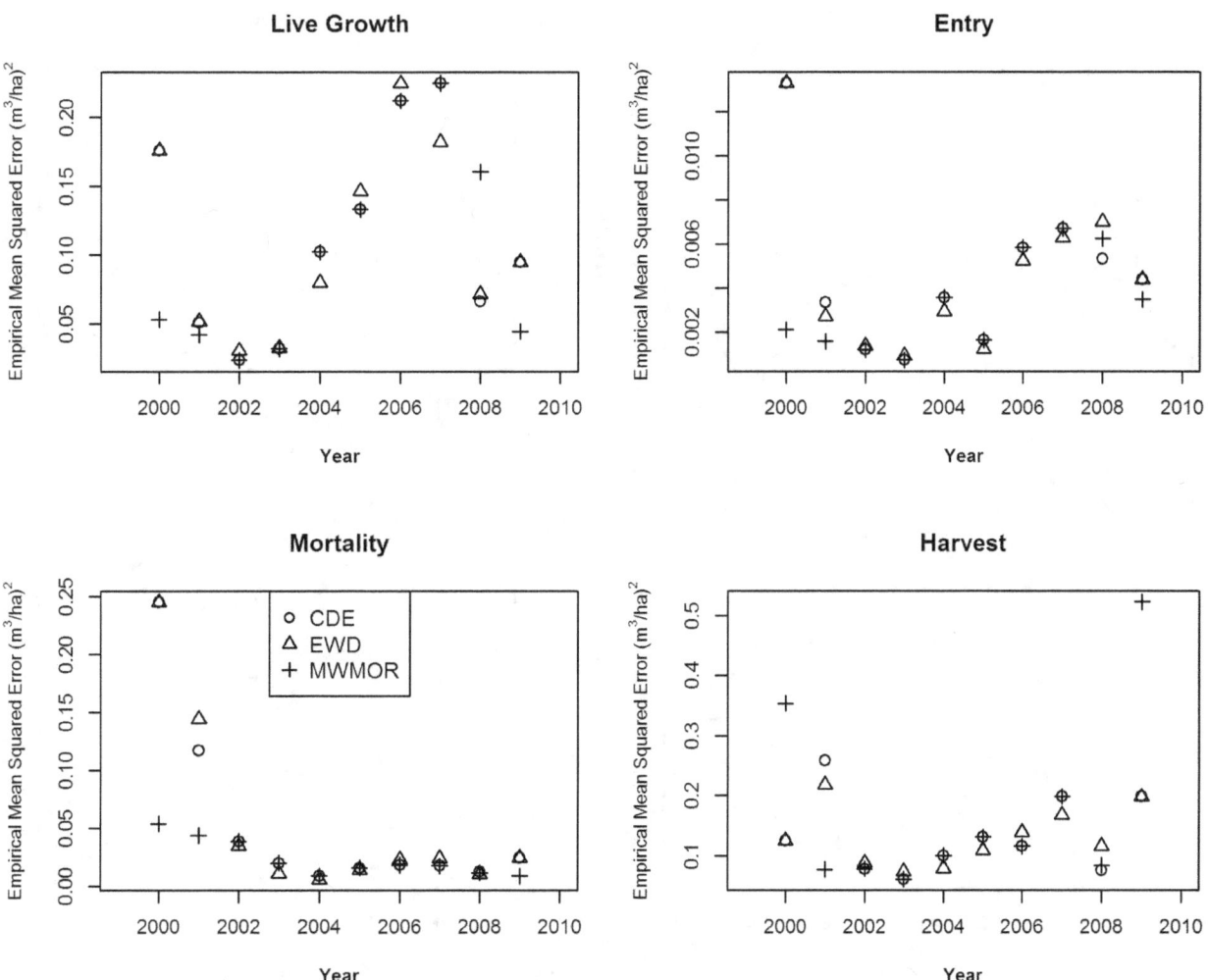

Figure 42E—The empirical mean squared error, over 1,000 iterations of 1,000 samples each from Population 4 under Sampling Error Structure 2, for the Centralized Difference Estimator (CDE), the Exponentially Weighted Difference (EWD) estimator, and the Moving-Windows Mean of Ratios (MWMOR) estimator, by growth component and estimation year.

Population 4 - Sample Error Structure 3

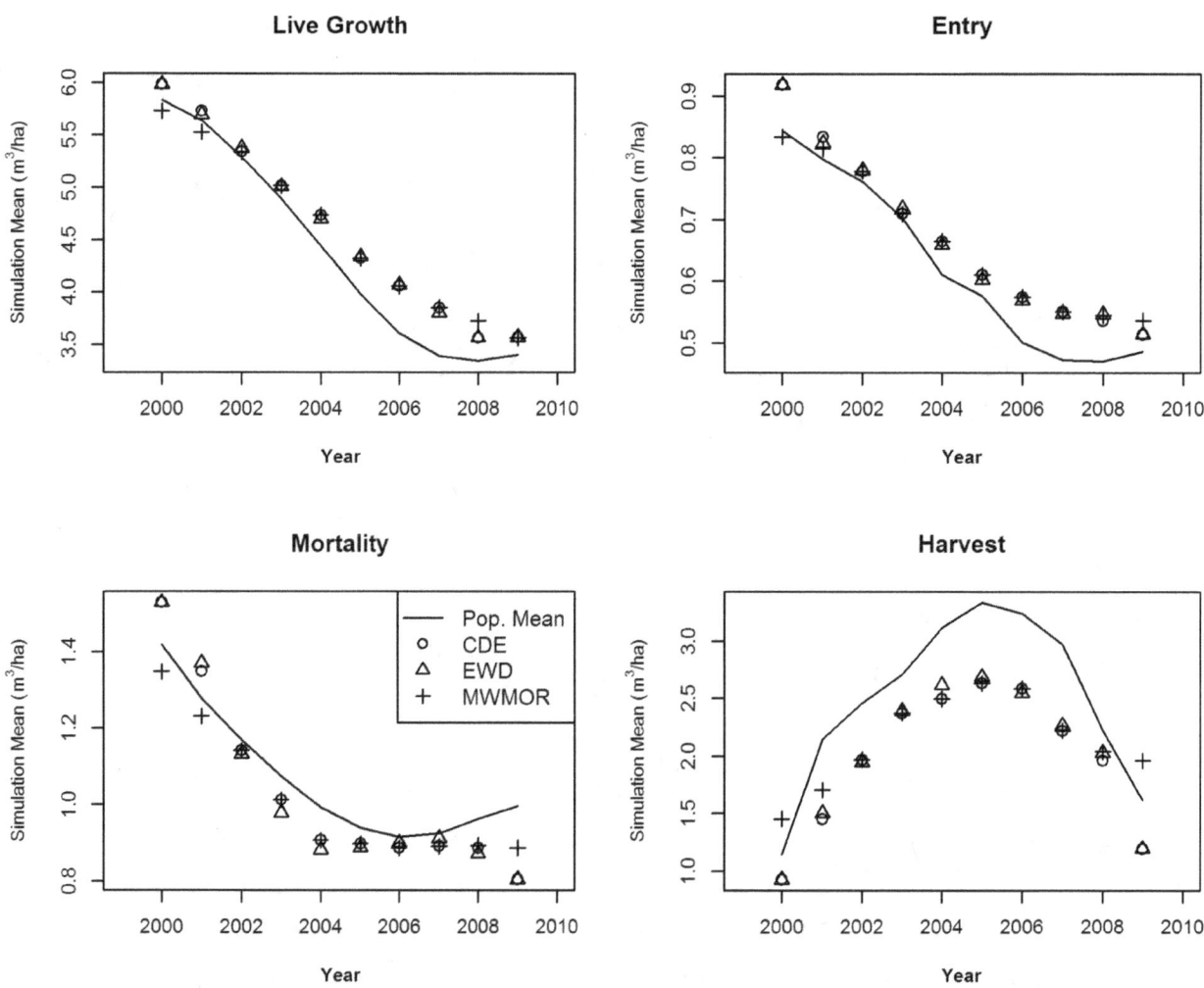

Figure 43M—The mean over 1,000 iterations of 1,000 samples each from Population 4 under Sampling Error Structure 3, for the Centralized Difference Estimator (CDE), the Exponentially Weighted Difference (EWD) estimator, and the Moving-Windows Mean of Ratios (MWMOR) estimator, by growth component and estimation year.

Population 4 - Sample Error Structure 3

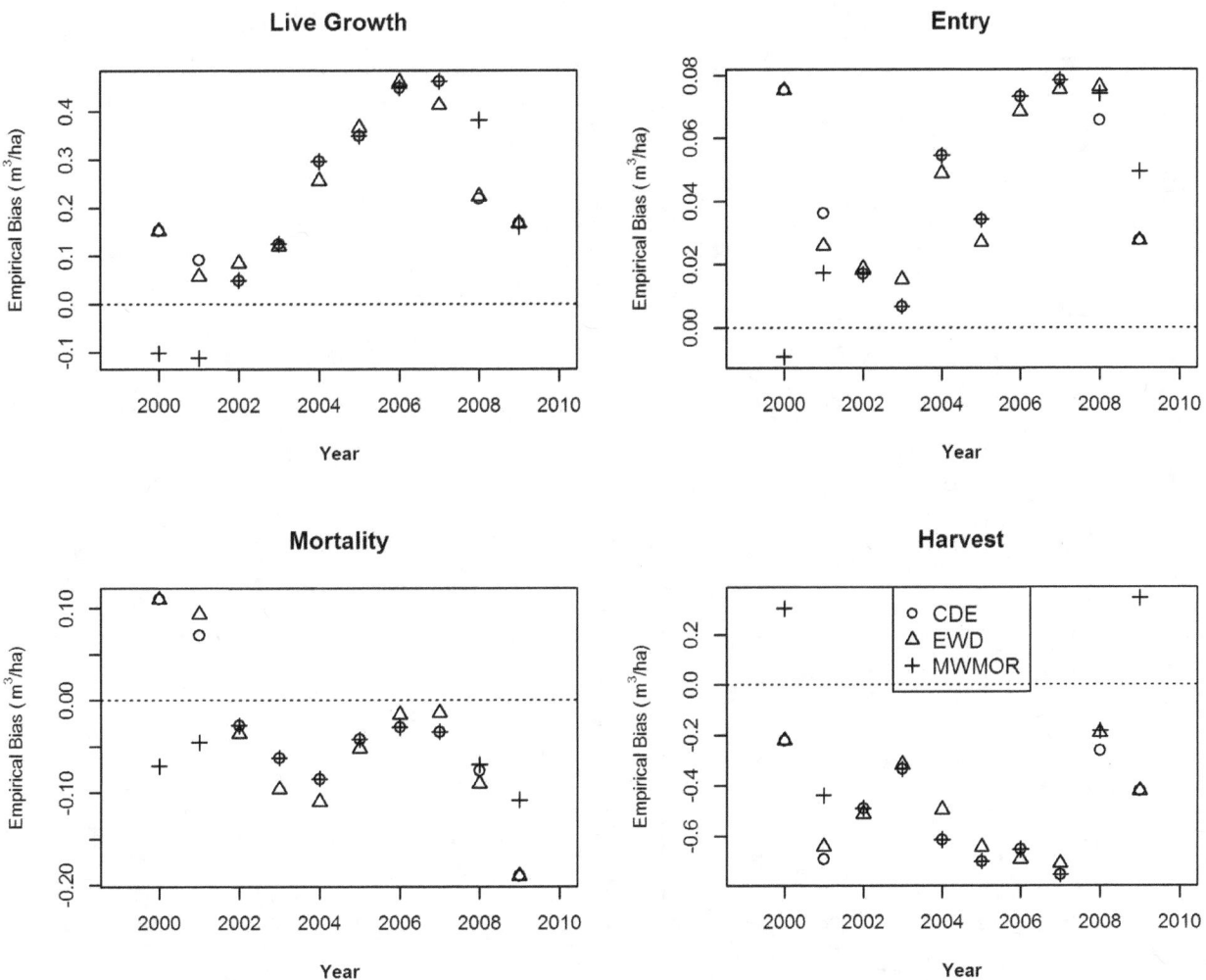

Figure 43B—The empirical bias, over 1,000 iterations of 1,000 samples each from Population 4 under Sampling Error Structure 3, for the Centralized Difference Estimator (CDE), the Exponentially Weighted Difference (EWD) estimator, and the Moving-Windows Mean of Ratios (MWMOR) estimator, by growth component and estimation year.

Population 4 - Sample Error Structure 3

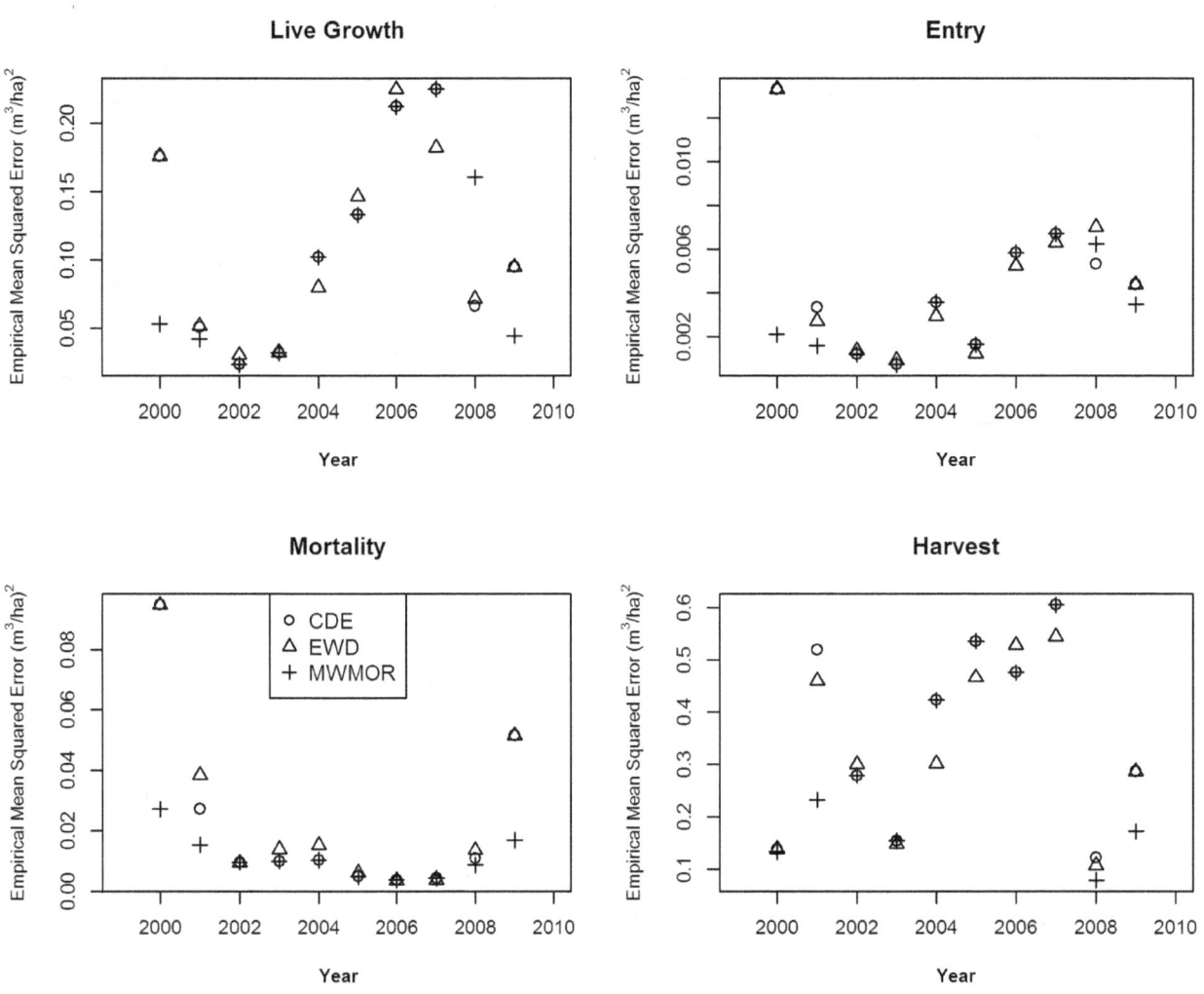

Figure 43E—The empirical mean squared error, over 1,000 iterations of 1,000 samples each from Population 4 under Sampling Error Structure 3, for the Centralized Difference Estimator (CDE), the Exponentially Weighted Difference (EWD) estimator, and the Moving-Windows Mean of Ratios (MWMOR) estimator, by growth component and estimation year.

Population 4 - Sample Error Structure 4

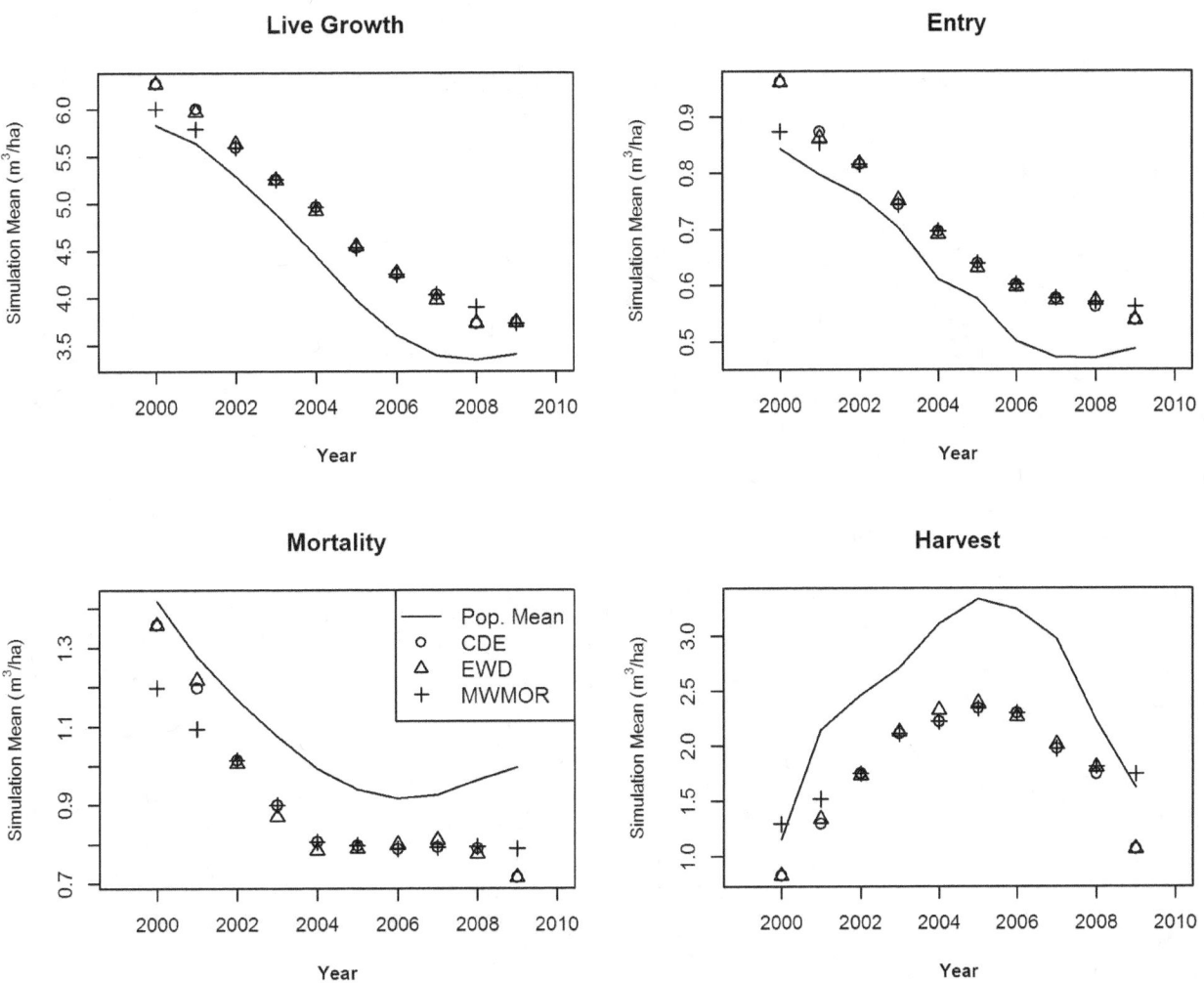

Figure 44M—The mean over 1,000 iterations of 1,000 samples each from Population 4 under Sampling Error Structure 4, for the Centralized Difference Estimator (CDE), the Exponentially Weighted Difference (EWD) estimator, and the Moving-Windows Mean of Ratios (MWMOR) estimator, by growth component and estimation year.

Population 4 - Sample Error Structure 4

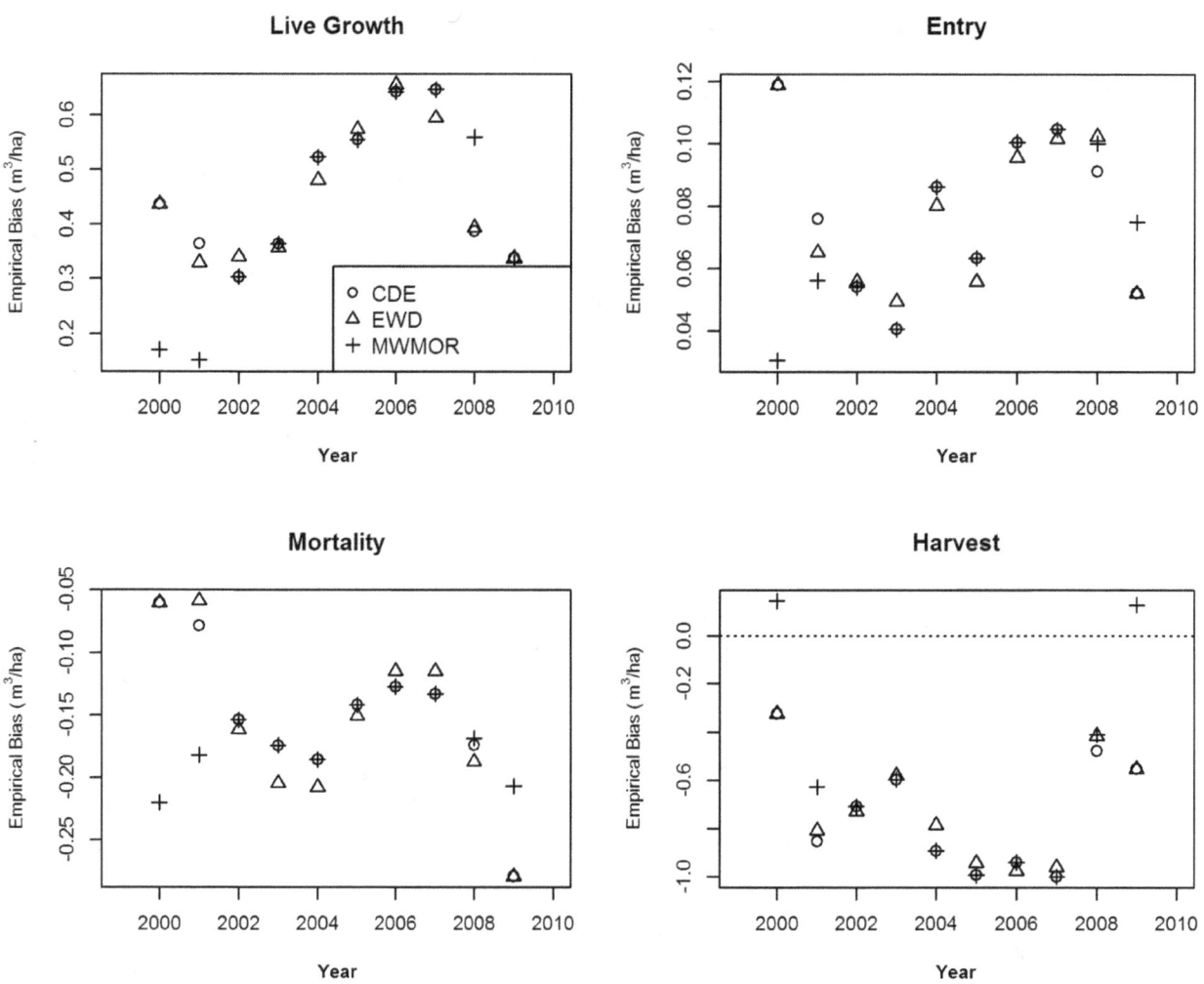

Figure 44B—The empirical bias, over 1,000 iterations of 1,000 samples each from Population 4 under Sampling Error Structure 4, for the Centralized Difference Estimator (CDE), the Exponentially Weighted Difference (EWD) estimator, and the Moving-Windows Mean of Ratios (MWMOR) estimator, by growth component and estimation year.

Population 4 - Sample Error Structure 4

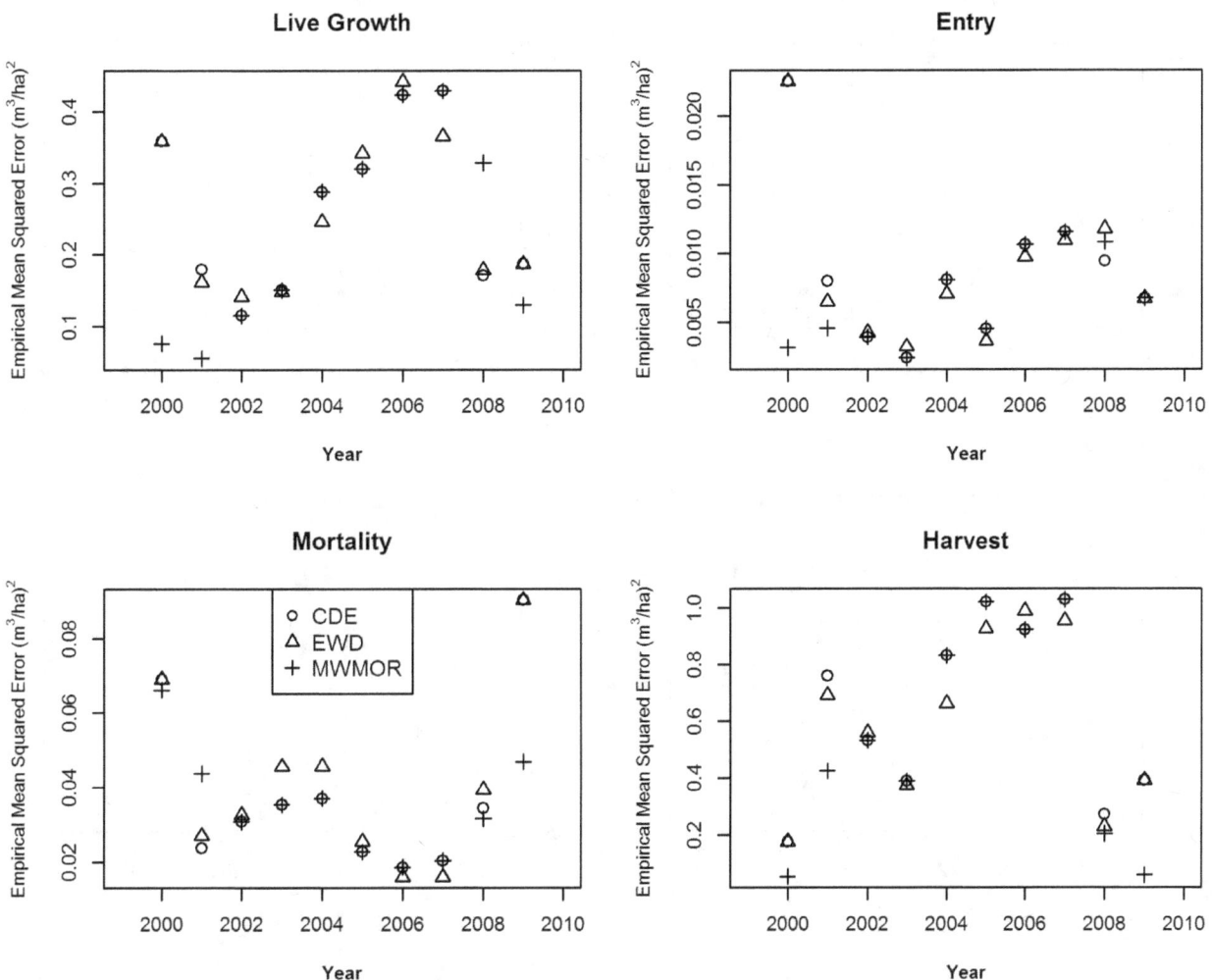

Figure 44E—The empirical mean squared error, over 1,000 iterations of 1,000 samples each from Population 4 under Sampling Error Structure 4, for the Centralized Difference Estimator (CDE), the Exponentially Weighted Difference (EWD) estimator, and the Moving-Windows Mean of Ratios (MWMOR) estimator, by growth component and estimation year.

Population 3 - Mortality

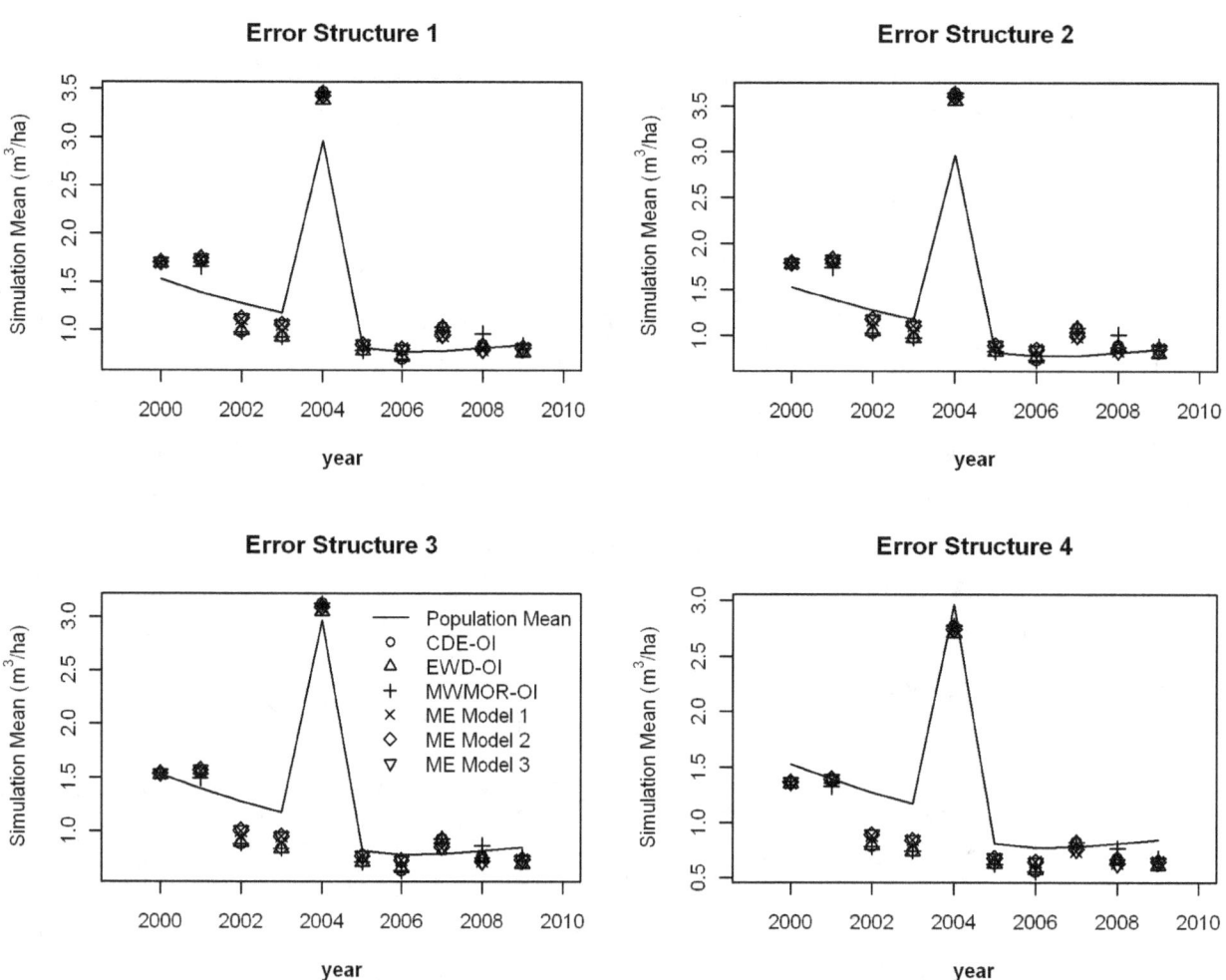

Figure 3MM—The mean over 1,000 iterations of 1,000 samples each from Population 3 under Sampling Error Structures 1 through 4, for the Mortality component by estimation year, for the estimators incorporating outside information (CDE-OI, EWD-OI, MWMOR-OI) and the Mixed Estimator (ME) under Models 1 through 3.

Population 3 - Mortality

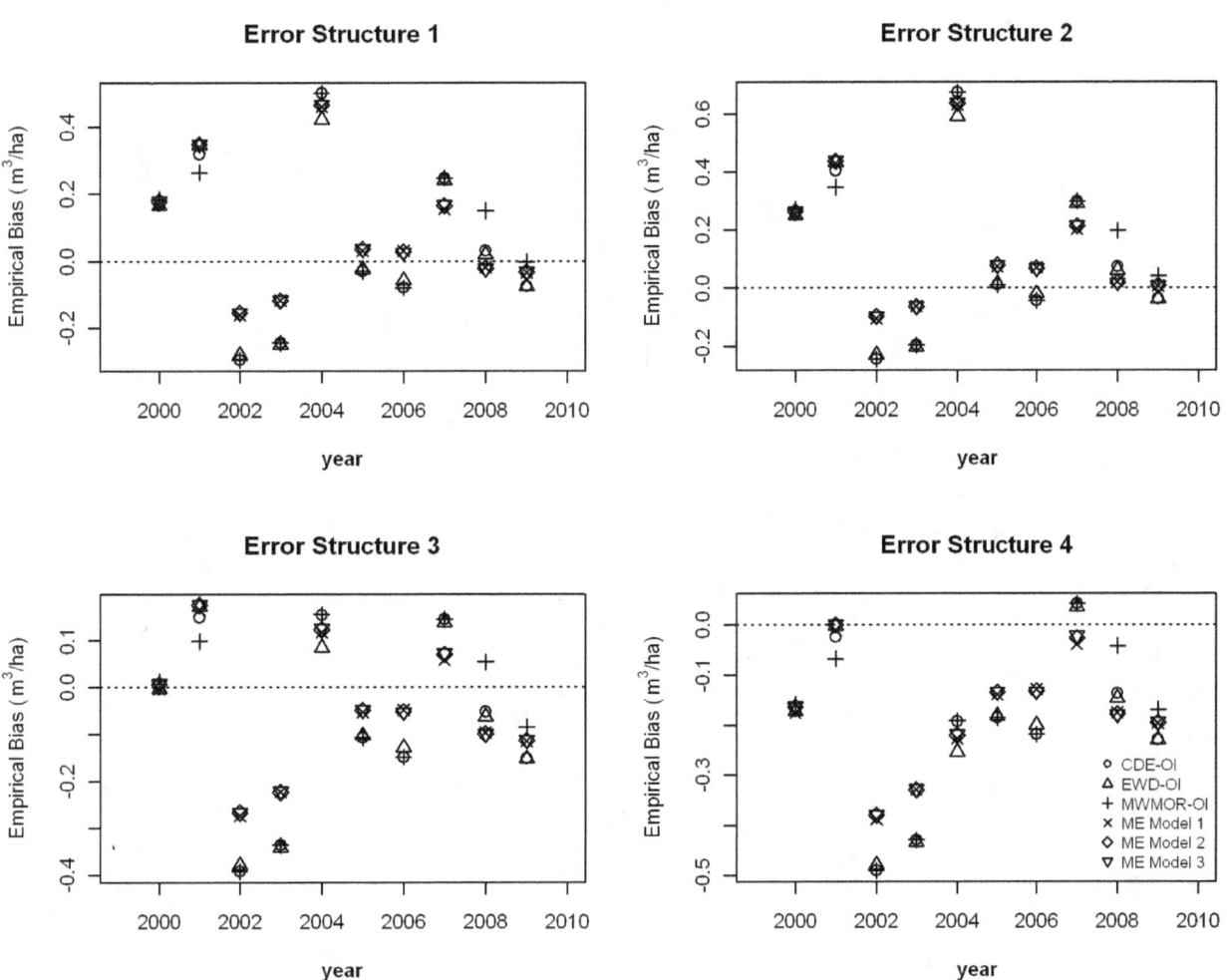

Figure 3MB—The empirical bias, over 1,000 iterations of 1,000 samples each from Population 3 under Sampling Error Structures 1 through 4, for the Mortality component by estimation year, for the estimators incorporating outside information (CDE-OI, EWD-OI, MWMOR-OI) and the Mixed Estimator (ME) under Models 1 through 3.

Population 3 - Mortality

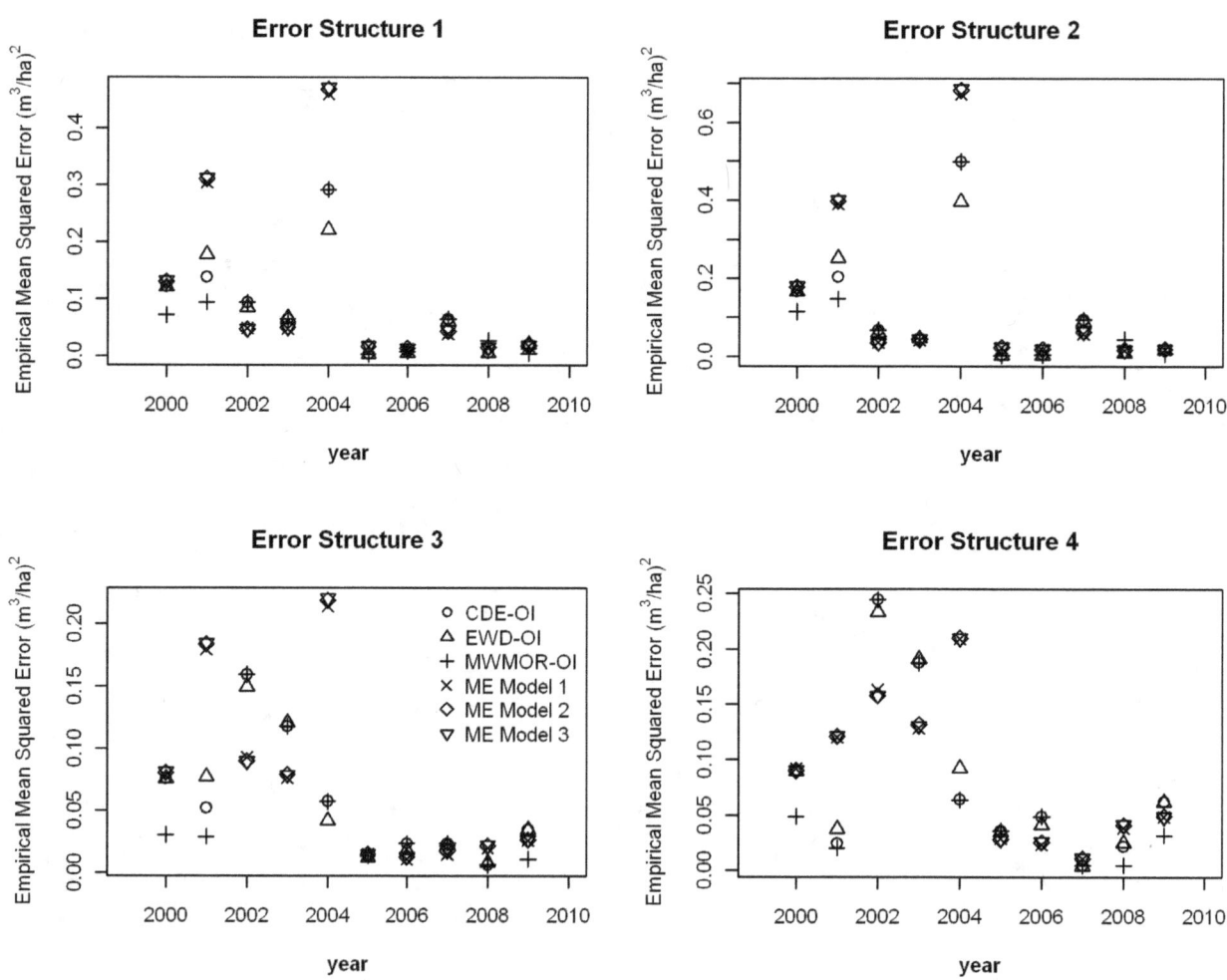

Figure 3ME—The empirical mean squared error, over 1,000 iterations of 1,000 samples each from Population 3 under Sampling Error Structures 1 through 4, for the Mortality component by estimation year, for the estimators incorporating outside information (CDE-OI, EWD-OI, MWMOR-OI) and the Mixed Estimator (ME) under Models 1 through 3.

ACKNOWLEGMENTS

This manuscript was improved by comments offered by Dr. James Westfall, U.S. Department of Agriculture Forest Service, Northern Research Station, and Dr. Christopher Oswalt, U.S. Department of Agriculture Forest Service, Southern Research Station.

LITERATURE CITED

Bechtold, W.A.; Patterson, P.L., eds. 2005. The enhanced Forest Inventory and Analysis Program—National Sampling Design and Estimation Procedures. Gen. Tech. Rep. SRS-GTR-80. Asheville, NC: U.S. Department of Agriculture Forest Service. 85 p.

Chandra, M.J. 2000. Statistical quality control. New York: CRC Press. 284 p.

Eastaugh, C.S.; Hasenauer, H. 2013. Biases in volume increment estimates derived from successive angle count sampling. Forest Science. 59(1): 1-14.

Eriksson, M. 1995. Compatible and time-additive change component estimators for horizontal-point-sampled data. Forest Science. 41(4): 796-822.

Gertner, G. 1987. Approximating precision in simulation projections: an efficient alternative to Monte Carlo methods. Forest Science. 33(1): 230-239.

Korhonen, K.T. 1993. Mixed estimation in calibration of volume functions of Scots pine. Silva Fennica. 27(4): 269-276.

Roesch, F.A. 2007a. Compatible estimators of the components of change for a rotating panel forest inventory design. Forest Science. 53(1): 50-61.

Roesch, F.A. 2007b. The components of change for an annual forest inventory design. Forest Science. 53(3): 406-413.

Roesch, F.A. 2014. Toward robust estimation of the components of forest population change. Forest Science. 60(2):000–000. http://dx.doi.org/10.5849/forsci.13-132. [Date accessed: January 23, 2014].

Roesch, F.A.; Van Deusen, P.C. 2012. Monitoring forest/non-forest land use conversion rates with annual inventory data. Forestry: An International Journal of Forest Research. 85(3): 391-398.

Roesch F.A.; Van Deusen, P.C. 2013. Time as a dimension of the sample design in national-scale forest inventories. Forest Science. 59(6): 610-622.

Theil, H. 1963. On the use of incomplete prior information in regression analysis. Journal of American Statistical Association. 58: 401-414.

Thomas, C.E.; Roesch, F.A. 1990. Basal area growth estimators for survivor component: a quality control approach. Southern Journal of Applied Forestry. 14(1): 12-18.

Van Deusen, P.C. 1996. Incorporating predictions into an annual forest inventory. Canadian Journal of Forest Research. 26: 1709-1713.

Van Deusen, P.C. 1999. Modeling trends with annual survey data. Canadian Journal of Forest Research. 29(12): 1824-1828.

Van Deusen, P.C. 2000. Alternative sampling designs and estimators for annual surveys. NC-GTR-212. In: Hansen, M.; Burk, T., eds. Integrated tools for natural resources inventories in the 21st century. St. Paul, MN: U.S. Department of Agriculture Forest Service, North Central Forest Experiment Station: 192-196.

Van Deusen, P.C.; Roesch, F.A. 2009. Estimating forest conversion rates with annual forest inventory data. Canadian Journal of Forest Research. 39(10): 1993–1996.

West, M.; Harrison, J. 1989. Bayesian forecasting and dynamic models. New York: Springer-Verlag. xxi + 704 p.

Roesch, Francis A. 2014. Toward robust estimation of the components of forest population change: simulation results. e-Gen. Tech. Rep. SRS-194. Asheville, NC: U.S. Department of Agriculture Forest Service, Southern Research Station. 79 p.

This report presents the full simulation results of the work described in Roesch (2014), in which multiple levels of simulation were used to test the robustness of estimators for the components of forest change. In that study, a variety of spatial-temporal populations were created based on, but more variable than, an actual forest monitoring dataset, and then those populations were sampled under four sets of sampling error structure. An estimator modification was shown, to be used when extraneously obtained information indicated that a deviation to the assumed population model existed. The extraneous information was also incorporated into a mixed estimator. The first three approaches, without the incorporation of extraneous information, are compatible with large monitoring efforts that require intervention-free results. The mixed estimation approach accounts for model assumptions that sometimes remain latent in other approaches and is amenable to the formal incorporation of the extraneously obtained information. All four approaches were shown to work well when the sampling error structure was unbiased, while some notable differences in performance were observed at the temporal extremities of observation, in the presence of temporal anomalies, and in the presence of biased sampling error structures. Only those results necessary to make the salient points were presented in Roesch (2014). Full results are presented here both for full disclosure and for the reader interested in a more detailed understanding of the effects of realistic sampling errors on temporal estimates.

Key Words: Annual inventories, components of change, forest monitoring, sampling error, spatial-temporal sample design.

How do you rate this publication?

Scan this code to submit your feedback or go to
www.srs fs.usda.gov/pubeval

www.ingramcontent.com/pod-product-compliance
Lightning Source LLC
Chambersburg PA
CBHW080321290526
45790CB00005B/2138